W9-CPH-442

THE BOOK OF NURTURING

◆

NINE
NATURAL LAWS FOR
ENRICHING
YOUR
FAMILY LIFE

L
I
N
D
A

and

R
I
C
H
A
R
D

E
Y
R
E

McGraw-Hill

New York / Chicago / San Francisco / Lisbon / London
Madrid / Mexico City / Milan / New Delhi / San Juan
Seoul / Singapore / Sydney / Toronto

All illustrations by Kvon.

1 2 3 4 5 6 7 8 9 0 DOC/DOC 0 9 8 7 6 5 4 3

ISBN 0-07-141506-8

McGraw-Hill books are available at special quantity discounts to use
as premiums and sales promotions, or for use in corporate training
programs. For more information, please write to the Director of
Special Sales, Professional Publishing, McGraw-Hill, Two Penn Plaza,
New York, NY 10121-2298. Or contact your local bookstore.

This book is printed on recycled, acid-free paper
containing a minimum of 50% recycled, de-inked fiber.

Library of Congress Cataloging-in-Publication Data
Eyre, Richard M.
      The book of nurturing : nine natural laws for enriching your
family life / Richard and Linda Eyre.
         p. cm.
      ISBN 0-07-141506-8
1. Child rearing. 2. Parenting. 3. Parent and child. I. Eyre,
      Linda. II. Title.
      HQ769.E984 2003
649'.1—dc21

                                                        2002156426

To

our children and their children

CONTENTS

CONTENTS

9
The Nature of
FREEDOM

THE LAW OF THE FLEAS

Keep fleas in a box long enough and they'll never jump above lid level,
even when the lid is gone.
Families should be about freedom and empowerment,
not about boxes and lids.

Closing
The Subconscious and the Symbolic

As we form good subconscious habits and
use the common language of symbols with our children,
we create a nurturing atmosphere, and
our houses become homes.

Introduction
SEQUEL OR PREQUEL?

SOMETHING MORE BASIC
THAN VALUES

A book on family or parenting had not topped the *New York Times* Bestseller List since the '50s (Dr. Spock's *Baby and Child Care*), so when our book *Teaching Your Children Values* reached that lofty position, all we could do was take a deep breath and wonder why. It was certainly not the best parenting book in 50 years, nor were we even close to being the best writers. Looking back, and being candid, there were probably two key reasons for the book's success.

Reason one was the title and the times. Values was the most urgent need parents felt in the '90s. As they watched wanton violence, recreational sex, and all kinds of instant gratification and other negative values devour their children, parents couldn't resist a guide for teaching basic values like honesty, self-discipline, and respect.

Reason two was Oprah. We'd promoted the book on plenty of other national talk shows, but it was Oprah who put the two of us and six of our children on her show for a full hour and explored each of the 12 values in the book and the methods by which parents could teach them. Having our kids on with us was a frightening experience—live television being watched by 20 million people—and our two youngest, who had never in their lives gone a full hour without fighting, were seated right next to each other! But we got through it, and by the next day bookstores couldn't keep the book on the shelves.

So that's a success story, right? Book sells millions and helps countless parents and families. Well . . . sort of. We've had a gratifying number of letters and e-mail from grateful parents. But we've also had our share of disturbing letters—discouraged messages from parents saying that while the values and the methods for teaching them sounded great, they were having big-time difficulty teaching them to their children. The reasons parents put forth for their failures made us realize that there are things even more basic than values that parents need to establish within their families. We got comments like:

"We don't communicate. They don't listen to me."

"My kids are never around. They'd rather be anywhere but home."

"I don't have the time."

"It just takes too much commitment."

"My kids make fun of the whole idea."

"They think I'm out of touch—they don't respect me."

"Everyone's just too cynical and too critical."

"My kids don't feel any accountability or responsibility."

"We never even see one another."

"He thinks I'm just criticizing him and that I don't trust him."

"We're just stuck; we can't change who we are or the patterns and habits we're in."

"I don't even know what they're doing or where they are at night—and they won't tell me."

"How do I teach values to a son who does drugs and belongs to a gang?"

"I only see my kids on the weekend—there's no continuity or consistency."

"If I try to force values, she'll think I don't accept her for who she is."

The feedback scared us—and woke us up. It reminded us of how incredibly difficult parenting is today and how many parents are at their wits' end, with no influence or sway or even any basic trust or relationship with their kids . . . and how many other parents are headed for that situation and don't even know that's where things are going.

Still other parents, perhaps the majority, are doing reasonably well but are feeling a deep need to more firmly establish the patterns of trust, support, and responsibility that will keep their family together and give their children the maximum chance for happiness and success. These parents want to establish an *offense* while their children are young so they don't have to constantly be setting up a *defense* when their children are older.

The bottom line is that there are some universal family needs, some basic principles of nurturing, even more fundamental than values, and that they must precede and prepare the way for the teaching of values. Principles like caring, commitment, consistency, and communication must be in place to create a home atmosphere in which teaching methods will work and values can be taught. These are principles of nurturing and of loving that make children feel secure, valued, and cherished and make them susceptible to the values we hope to teach them.

At one point, when *Teaching Your Children Values* was selling so well and seemed to be helping so many families, we considered writing a sequel. But as we thought about it and read our mail, we realized that what we really needed to write was a *prequel*—a more basic book that addressed the more basic needs of families—a book about establishing the atmosphere that turns a house into a home and creates the nurturing environment that enables values to be taught and learned.

There is an old adage that says, "People don't care how much you know until they know how much you care." A similar truth applies to parenting. We can't really teach our children until we've learned to nurture them. In that sense, this book is truly a prequel, because its lessons of nurturing should precede and prepare the way for the values we want to teach our children. Said another way: *Before we can teach our children true values, we have to truly value our children.*

ARE YOU ORGANIZING OR NURTURING?

So many parents today have become better at organizing their kids than at nurturing them. Organizing is something we do with our brains. It's about finishing homework and getting to soccer or music lessons on time. It's about helping our children do all they can do and be all they can be; and it ranges from getting them in the right preschool when they're three years old to getting them into the right college when they're eighteen.

But with all our organizing, have we done enough nurturing? Nurturing is something we do with our hearts as well as our heads. It's about adding the hug to the schedule, the praise to the push, the warmth to the light. It's about noticing who they already are as we help them toward what they can become.

The worst parenting metaphor we've ever heard goes something like this: "The child is the lump of clay, and the parent is the sculptor." Children are anything but lumps, and parents who try to mold them into enhancements of their own status, or into extensions of their own egos, will fail—and will do real harm to their children in the process.

A vastly better analogy is that of a seedling. The tiny green shoots in the greenhouse nursery may all look alike, yet one is an oak, one a pine, one an apple tree. We don't mold them, we nurture them, discovering who they are, learning what they need, providing the individually appropriate amounts of water, sunshine, and fertilizer to help them grow into the best of what they already are.

Organizing, molding, guiding, and teaching all have their place, but *nurturing* is the ongoing blanket under which the best aspects of each can occur. And the seedling analogy is just the beginning of what nature can teach us about nurturing.

STORIES AND ANALOGIES: A WAY TO REMEMBER AND TO APPLY

This book contains nine simple but powerful "natural laws" of nurturing that can protect and improve families and give children a sense of worth and esteem. But no matter how basic or important any law or principle is, it's hard to remember it and consistently apply it day after day. So we suggest dramatizing or connecting the laws and principles to stories or fables—some sort of symbol that makes it live in our minds and resonate in our hearts so we can put it into practice automatically, naturally, even subconsciously.

When we first started presenting the nine basic principles of this book in lectures or seminars, there were no symbols or animal stories connected to them. We just put each one up on a screen with a big "number 1" or "number 2." We explained each of the nine principles and gave examples of how it could work in a family. Parents in our audiences nodded heads and looked impressed. Yet after the seminars, when we asked parents how many of the nine they could remember, the average "score" was four. And if parents could only remember a few of them right after our lecture, how many would they be able to think of and actually apply in the real world of their real lives?

One night in a seminar, we told an "animal story"—a simple incident about humpback whales and how they're capable of hearing the song of another humpback hundreds of miles away. The need to listen—the listening or "communication principle"—was the one that every parent could remember at the end of the evening, and they were clear that when listening is hard or "distant," it's the most important time to tune in and really hear. We had the feeling that those parents would not only remember that point, but would remember to implement it. Furthermore, *children* could learn and remember that principle because of the animal metaphor that went with it.

We began to think about the importance and power of symbols, of how they can help us stay focused on what really matters and help us make good choices even when we're under pressure.

Then, drawing on some personal experiences and on the remarkable characteristics of some of nature's creatures, we created an animal story or fable for each of the other eight principles. Drawing on the instinct of crabs to pull one another back rather than boost one another up, the "Positive Support Principle" became the "Law of the Crabs." The "Commitment Principle" became the "Law of the Geese," and the "Tough Love Principle" became the "Law of the Elephant's Trunk." It's easier to learn and to remember from analogies based on the positive or negative behavior of other creatures. And, since nature itself is a nourishing, nurturing place, that is the best environment or arena from which to draw our analogies.

So . . . this is not a heavy book of complicated theories or ponderous analysis. It's a graphic, focused, and simple book about nine basic but profound laws or lessons of nurturing. The animal stories and illustrations are intended to productively and positively *simplify* the lessons—not in the sense of making them simple-minded, but to make them simple for the mind to use. As Oliver Wendell Holmes said: "I would not give a fig for the simplicity this side of complexity, but I would give my life for the simplicity on the other side of complexity."

The nine animal stories or natural laws are the *distillation* of powerful and far-reaching principles. While the basic idea of each is simple and obvious, the *details* of each story are designed to show how each principle works and what each one requires of us. For example, it's not just that humpback whales *communicate*, it's that they communicate with special intensity in times of need, it's that they don't interrupt one another's songs, that their communication is almost always positive and approving, and that they virtually never lose touch with their family, or "pod."

Thus, the nine natural laws are the condensation, the concentration, the culmination of bigger parts of the universe. They are the fundamental principles through which we can effectively nurture our children, and make our houses into homes. The fables or stories that illustrate and illuminate the laws are "memory magnets" that will hold them in our hearts, where they will hopefully become strong commitments, and in our minds, where they will eventually become good habits.

THE
NATURAL NATURE
OF NURTURING
The Intelligent Application
of Love

We have never met a parent who didn't love his or her child. But we've met plenty of parents (and sometimes *been* the kind of parents) who didn't *apply* their love in very intelligent ways. Some parents try to love their children by spoiling them, or by letting them do whatever they want, or by lecturing them, or by overdisciplining them, or by forcing them into the mold of what they have projected them to be.

As you already know from the title and the introduction, we feel the word *nurturing* takes parental love to a higher level. It's a cozy, comfortable word that all parents seem to identify with. It represents a quality and a skill that most parents want to develop. It can be a verb depicting one of the most important things we do in life, or an adjective by which most parents would like to be described. Doing nurturing well empowers the child and calms and relieves or diminishes a parent's stress. Nurturing is also the domain of grandparents, aunts and uncles, godparents, mentors, teachers, and all who love and are committed to a child.

Webster's dictionary defines *nurturing* with words like "training," "educating," and "nourishing." Also: ". . . the process of raising or bringing up" and ". . . moral training and discipline." For the purpose of this book, we would like to define nurturing as "the warm and wise application of love." Let's go even further and agree that we want to nurture our children in ways that give them gifts of family security and identity, and of individual confidence and uniqueness, and that open them to a sense of responsibility and empowerment that will maximize their chances of reaching their fullest potential and fulfillment.

To do all this, our nurturing must be deep and honest as well as intelligent. This is a book about the *nature* of nurturing, about the qualities and patterns parents and other relatives and mentors of children can develop to create an atmosphere that nurtures and nourishes the children they love. We call these qualities and patterns the "Natural Laws of Nurturing." There are nine of them, and they deal with the most fundamental things of all, things like commitment, praise, responsibility, security, discipline, and communication.

CREATING
YOUR OWN "PARENTING NATURE"

Since the nine principles and the stories that illustrate them come from *nature,* they are *natural* laws. Once they're thoroughly understood they are comfortably remembered and instinctive and easy to apply. With sincere and well-intentioned parents (the kind who buy parenting books), the natural laws will resonate as they're read. Their animal symbols will remind us even when we begin to forget. If we're interrupting more than we're listening, we'll think of the whales. If we're criticizing more than praising, we'll think of the crabs. The stories can work on us—or in us—until doing the right thing feels natural and doing the wrong thing feels wrong.

Remember, as you read, that it is the laws or principles that matter. The fables or animal stories are there only to help us remember the laws; the stories were created as memory pegs. The principles precipitated the stories, not the other way around. We didn't watch crabs or listen to whales or look up at redwood trees and say, "Wow, there's a lesson in this for parents." Rather, we started with nine principles that we've grown to feel are the most important lessons parents can learn, the nine pillars on which good parenting and successful families rest, things we've been talking to parents about for 20 years. As ways to remember and internalize them, we found or created the nine stories or animal allegories.

We're not Aesopian fable writers—we're family and parenting writers trying to make it easier for good parents to remember to do the right things. But speaking of Aesop, we have used his most famous tale—the tortoise and the hare—in this book. Another of his fables—the scorpion and the frog—gets us back to the question of "nature."

> The scorpion asks the frog to swim him across a river.
>
> "No, you might sting me," says the frog.
>
> "I will not," says the scorpion, "because if I did, we could both drown and die."
>
> Persuaded, the frog agrees to give him a ride. Halfway across the river, the scorpion stings him. As he flounders and they both begin to drown, the frog asks, "Why did you do it?"
>
> "Because," says the scorpion, "it is my nature."

People too, particularly parents, sometimes blame their nature for a lot of what they do. We know one sad man who cheated on his wife (and thus on his children) for years, and the best defense he could come up with was that his father and grandfather were philanderers—and that he was therefore genetically disposed toward adultery. As absurd as that sounds, there are some negative or destructive things on which most of us catch ourselves emulating our parents, whether we want to or not. We notice ourselves treating and speaking to our children just as our parents did to us, and saying things we vowed we would never say in tones we vowed we would never use.

The word *nature* is interesting. Much of our nature or instinct or natural inclination as parents is very good. We have a nature to nurture, to care for and to give the best to our children. But we also find ourselves disposed to criticize, sometimes to discipline too harshly, sometimes to spoil and pamper too much.

Subconsciously, each of us has learned lessons of parenting all our lives, some good and some bad—from our own parents, from other families we've been around or read about, from our own disposition and inclination, even from the advice and clichés we've heard from "experts."

The goal of the nine laws that follow is to help you design and create your own *chosen* parenting nature, using nature stories to help you remember the kind of parent you want to be. Then maybe someday someone will ask you a very different question than the one the frog asked the scorpion, but you will give exactly the same answer. "How did you raise such an outstanding child?" You'll probably reply only in your heart: "It's my nature."

1

The Nature of COMMITMENT

Near the small town in Idaho where I (Linda) grew up, there's a bird refuge that is frequented in the warmer months by Canadian geese. I first remember being aware of the big birds each fall when I heard their distant honking and looked up to see their perfect V formations high above me, heading south. I learned from biology lectures and textbooks that in their yearly migration, geese fly high enough to find the jet streams; that they fly in a V formation to cut wind resistance, taking turns in the taxing position at the front of the V; and that they can fly thousands of miles without coming down. I also learned that by some kind of inner biological radar or global positioning, they return in the spring to the precise spot from which they left, the spot where they were born, their home.

A couple of times in the early spring, I think I saw the actu-al moment when some of the geese returned to our bird refuge. They swooped in looking exhausted but delighted to be home, landing smoothly on the water and noisily and joyously paddling around as though they were opening a house that had been closed for the winter.

As much as I enjoyed those spring and fall glimpses of migra-tion, it was the early summer that became my favorite season for geese watching. When one of my parents drove me through the marshlands, we would see the fluffy brown babies paddling along in a line behind their mother with their father always swim-ming close by in watchful protection. If it was windy or stormy, the mother would slow down and look back as if counting and keeping track, and the father would move into closer formation to help any that might stray. When the babies tried to climb out onto a steep bank, both Mom and Dad would help boost them up.

When I got older, further research taught me that Canadian geese parents not only work together, they stay together, mating for life and living as long as 60 or 70 years. They stay with their children too, until they are grown, their love beautifully illus-trated by their habits.

One day as we drove through the marsh, we saw a mature female who at first we thought was hurt. She was making a lot of noise and swimming frantically and erratically. As we watched, we realized that she had lost one of her babies. She had her other tiny goslings grouped together on a bank and she would check on them and then dart off into the various passages through the marsh grass, looking for the missing one. We thought her loud, frequent honks were calls for the lost chick, but she looked up as she called and we realized she was calling for her mate. A moment later he swooped in. Together they found the missing chick, then hovered over it until it was reintegrated into the family. Whatever it was that he'd been doing, the dad left it immediately when his family needed him. After that minor goose family crisis, both parents swam busily from chick to chick, nuzzling and clucking to them incessantly, as if to reassure them beyond doubt that they would be cared for and never lost or forgotten.

I recently read of a similar experience with a family of geese trying to cross a road. A driver came upon a father goose who had walked to the middle of the road, turned to face potential oncoming traffic, and spread his wings wide like a crossing guard. Then the mother and children began to cross. The driver, who had pulled to a stop, said she could see that the father goose was not watching her car but actually looking into her eyes to see if she was going to move toward them. When he was sure she was not, he left his sentinel position to hurry the rest of his struggling kids across the road.

Maybe it was because of the simplicity and beauty of that childhood setting and the memories I have there, but I came to love those Canadian geese and to be awed by how far they could travel and yet always come home. To me, they came to represent *the commitment of families—parents who do their best to stay together, who reassure their children of their commitment to them, who help and guide, who are predictably where they're supposed to be, and whose children in turn learn to be committed to their own future families.*

The Law of the Geese is commitment and priority. Commitment by married spouses to each other. Deep commitment by married or single parents to their children. And the clear and consistent prioritizing of children and family above all other priorities.

The trust, security, and confidence that we all want our children to feel comes directly from the open and obvious commitment of parents, and from children knowing they are our first priority and that they matter more to us than anything else. Once children feel this—deeply and truly feel it—they will forgive us for our mistakes, for our tempers, for our inconsistencies, for all our inadequacies as parents.

We need to remind ourselves that our children do not automatically know of our commitment and of their priority. Children's natural tendencies are often toward insecurity rather than security, and toward doubt and guilt rather than confidence. We need to tell them more often of our total commitment and of how much more important they are to us than anything else.

❖ ❖

L i k e   the geese, we must always come home.

L i k e   the geese, we must put our children first.

L i k e   the geese, we must let them know by what we say and what we do that they are our highest priority.

L i k e   the geese, we must understand that commitment is the most complete expression of love.

L i k e   the geese, we must frequently remind our children of our love and tell them of our commitment and loyalty to them.

L i k e   the geese, we must relish home and enjoy being there more than any other place.

❖ ❖

Animal allegories can help us understand and imprint a principle into our hearts and our heads, but we still need examples of how to apply the law, how to translate it into human terms and transform it into real-life family implementation. Each parent has to find his or her own individual ways to do this, but stories from other families can help. As a parent, you're usually the storyteller, but at this point in each chapter, let us tell you a couple of bedtime stories.

We know of one family that learned the lesson of priorities and commitment by accident (literally). We'll call the mother Emily, and this is her story.

Even though she was sitting at a stoplight, Emily could feel her heart racing. Her grip on the steering wheel tightened and she realized she was talking to herself: "Please let this be the last red light before I get there." Almost every day she found herself with more on her plate than she could possibly handle, and the self-talk seemed to help a little.

"I should have left the office 10 minutes earlier," she said to herself, "even if I hadn't finished the proposal. Timmy will be waiting on the curb by the soccer field again. The babysitter will be worried about being late for her aerobics class and trying to 'hold off' the baby until I can get there to nurse him. Alison and Jamie will be playing computer games instead of doing their homework and practicing the piano. What are we going to have for dinner? I haven't been to the grocery store in a week, and the girls have to be at their soccer practice in 45 minutes from right now!" She could feel her blood pressure rising.

Like a shot out of a cannon, Emily stepped on the gas the instant the light turned green, which would be her last big hurrying mistake for a long time. Another car, trying to beat the yellow light from Emily's right, plowed into her and everything went black.

When Emily opened her eyes, she was in a hospital bed. Her husband was holding her hand, and the children were all standing over her with scared, loving eyes. The babysitter was holding her happy, chubby baby, who was giggling at "funny mommy." The doctor was assuring her that, aside from a concussion that might blur her vision for a while and a broken ankle that would prevent her from driving for a month, she was going to be fine.

After the relief, Emily's first thought was panic. How can my family survive without me being able to drive . . . or even to see? How can I keep juggling everything if I'm not at full strength?

As the days passed, however, even though her vision wasn't very clear, her life began to focus. Something about an accident that could have killed her helped Emily get her life into sharper view. She realized that she was overcommitted—to things that really wouldn't matter much 20 years from now.

"Sorry, honey," she said to her husband. "I guess I won't be going to work for a while. We'll have to cut back on some of our extras. I guess I'm just going to have to spend more time thinking about you!"

He smiled.

"Sorry kids," she began when she had their attention later that night at the dinner Jamie and Alison had helped prepare. Leg elevated, Emily announced, "We're just going to have to give up soccer for a while. Besides the fact that I can't drive, we haven't been eating dinner together. Some days it seems that we don't have time for anything but soccer and all the other music and sports lessons. We're even too tired for bedtime stories. It's hard to get homework done. We just can't keep trying to do everything. You're growing up! We have to make the most of every day we have together, and soccer three times a week for each of you just doesn't allow that."

Jamie, Timmy, and Alison glanced at one another, and then Alison spilled the beans: "It's okay, Mom, because none of us really likes soccer anyway."

Trying not to be too flabbergasted about all the time she'd spent in the thick of thin things, Emily was jarred into a new realization. The time spent together when the children are in the home is short . . . too short to waste by continually being overcommitted to nonessential things. What really matters, she realized, is being together and making our commitment more obvious and visible. A broken ankle made it easier, because it cut out some of the nonessentials and refocused everyone on one another, reminding Emily and her husband that whenever we trade time for things, it's a bad deal, and that a little downtime with our kids is worth more than all the uptime of trying to do everything.

Years ago, living in Washington, D.C., we knew a struggling young family who attended the same church we did. The parents didn't make much money and lived with several small children in a tiny house with one bathroom. Despite their difficulties, the kids always seemed happy and well-adjusted. We moved away and lost contact with them. Many years later, I (Richard) was giving a guest lecture at a university. A lovely freshman coed came up afterward and introduced herself. She was one of those children. As we talked, I was impressed with her poise and self-confidence.

I asked her a little about her childhood. "What did your parents do? What were their parenting methods?"

She laughed. "You remember my parents," she said. "They were scrambling just to keep food on the table. They didn't have much time for parenting methods or techniques." Then she paused and her face became serious, her eyes a little misty. "I'll tell you one thing, though—they let us know that we were what mattered." She told me how her dad used to tuck her in bed and then take her face in both of his hands and look deep into her eyes and say, "I love you honey. You are my first priority. I am completely committed to your mom and to you kids. And I always will be." She said she never tired of it. Being away from home, she said she could still hear those words in her head and that they warmed her even now.

The frequent *expression* of commitment is almost as important as the possession of it. We should guard against becoming like stoic "Alf and Anna" of the old country. Anna says, "Alf, you never tell me you love me," and Alf replies, "Anna, I told you I loved you 30 years ago on the day we were married, and if anything ever changes, you'll be the first to know."

Learn the Law of the Geese. Make your commitment obvious and let your spouse and your children bask in the security it will give them.

❖ ❖

At this point in each chapter, we'll look at some brief snapshots of families trying to apply the natural law in their everyday living. Some of these brief glimpses are from our own family; many are from families we have met or corresponded with over the years; still others combine the ideas of two or more different families. All the snapshots begin with the word *one*, suggesting that one parent can make a difference; that if *one* family can do it, so can you; that *each* family is unique and individual and what worked for one family might not work for you, but might stimulate a related idea for your *one* family. A picture is worth a thousand words, and some of these little "snapshots" may give you ideas or inspire you to try similar things. Don't try them all! Just pick those that appeal to you or that you feel would "work" with your situation. Let them prompt your own ideas. The point is to show how many ways there are to work on and implement each principle.

One family with elementary-school-age children, in a simple effort to make commitment more obvious and constant, decided together on something called "commitment hugs." It was a simple, two-part idea: (1) That they would give one another more physical hugs (the goal was at least one per day from each to each), and (2) that the unspoken message of each hug (to be consciously thought of every time a hug was given or received) was, "I am committed to you as my highest priority. You matter to me more than anything else and I love you." They even had a calligrapher put the commitment hug message on a plaque that they hung in their kitchen.

One dad whose work required a lot of travel decided to call his two adolescent daughters every single evening that he was gone to ask about their day, to tell them he was thinking of them and that they were more important to him than his work—in fact, that the *reason* for work was to support them and their mother.

One aunt of two small children—of a single mother who worked full-time six days a week and who had a hard time expressing her love—decided to take some of the nurturing needs into her own hands. She stopped by their day-care facility a couple of times a week during her lunch hour and spent the time holding and cuddling the children and telling them how much both she *and* their mother loved them. On Sundays she'd stop by and help her sister take the kids to the zoo or a park and take the lead in telling the kids how much they were loved and how much she and their mother thought about them each day.

One father, in the middle of some important projects at his office, was feeling guilty for getting home late most nights, after his seven-year-old daughter was already in bed. He explained to the girl that the late nights wouldn't last too long and that in the meantime she could have a secret password to call him. The password was "Number one" because she was the most important person to him. She knew his office number, and when she called, she was to just say "Number one," and the secretary would either find her dad right then or put her on the message list as the number one or very first person her dad would call back.

One couple decided to try to reserve Monday nights for some kind of family activity with their three small children, even if it was just a quick trip to the ice cream store. They liked to say—to their kids, as often as possible—"First weeknight for the first priority," and they tried to let the children decide where to go and what to do.

They also taught their four- and six-year-olds the words "commitment" (defined as a promise) and "priority" (defined as a very important thing). The kids felt cool using "big words," even if it wasn't always in the context their parents had in mind: "But mom, that candy bar is a priority, and you committed I could have it."

One busy working mom just made a rule for herself that she wouldn't fill in her daily "to do" list until she had asked herself, "What do my children need today?" Even if it were just a little thing, she felt better having thought about it first, before the many challenges and demands of the day.

One family decided to quit saying good-bye on the phone or when someone left for work or school. Instead, they just said, "Love you."

One couple officially "remarried"—holding a second ceremony later in their lives to repeat and reemphasize their marriage vows and commitments to each other and to their children. They wrote out "commitment documents" to each other (which they also shared with the children). Part of the husband's read like this:

> I hereby recommit myself, my resources, my gifts, and my soul to you as my highest priority, as my wife, and as the only romantic love of my life. While I am far from perfect as a husband, there are many things you can absolutely and always count on from me. One is that I will put you and your interests first in every choice or decision I face. Two is that I will always be completely honest with you and have no secrets from you. Third is that I will be a full partner with you in the raising of our children. Fourth is that I will never let other priorities (work, sports, etc.) get ahead of you and the kids or cause me to do anything that would damage or impact negatively on you or on your happiness. Fifth is that I will remember and keep our marriage vows.

One single dad who worked on an auto assembly line made arrangements to bring his third-grade son to the factory one Saturday when the line was closed. He explained how the cars were assembled and showed the boy what he did on each one. Then he took his son to the end of the assembly line and showed him the finished cars. "Son," he said, "cars are pretty important, especially when you're going down the freeway. But you are a thousand times more important to me than all these cars. The reason I come here to work is so I can pay for the food and clothes and other things you need. You are what really matters to me. Don't ever forget that!"

One couple noticed how their small daughter's face lit up when she saw the two of them showing open affection toward each other. They began to make a point of holding hands or hugging and kissing while the little girl was watching, and then going over and hugging their daughter and telling her how much they loved her.

One couple who had adopted three children made it a point at least once a month to tell their children how lucky they felt because they got to choose their children rather than just accepting whoever was born to them. The kids' insecurities and worries that their birth parents may not have wanted them were swallowed up with the love and commitment of their "forever" parents.

As you finish reading the snapshots about how "one" family did one thing or "one" mom or dad did another, take a few minutes to think about ways your family has tried to apply the Law of the Geese or about ways you might like to apply it. Write those ideas on the lines provided. If nothing comes to your mind right now, come back and fill this in later. Like all the other "snapshots," what you write will be about one family—your family. But instead of starting with the three-letter O-word "one," your paragraph will start with the three-letter O-word "our."

Our family

_____

_____

_____

_____

_____

_____

❖ ❖

As a final method, consider simply reading the abbreviated animal story to your child. Then talk about it together and see how well your child "gets it." At this point it may be helpful to focus on the drawing at the beginning of the chapter.

What We Learn from the Geese
❖

Beautiful, big Canadian geese teach us the
lesson of commitment.
They mate for life, sometimes spending
more than 50 years together
before one of them dies.
They are completely committed to their families.
They help each other. They do things together.
They keep each other safe.
They know they can depend on each other.
They put each other first. They always come home.
Our family can be just like that.
Let's remind one another to be like the geese.

*T*he particular methods we use to show our commitment—
to remind ourselves and our families that they are our priorities—are not as important as the simple fact that we *do* it, and
do it often. As they grow up, children who feel our commitment will talk to us more, listen to us more, and trust us more.
The constant reestablishment of commitment is the natural law
that creates the atmosphere and the environment where the
other eight laws have the best chance of flourishing.

Why let spouses and children *assume* our love when it's so easy to *tell* them? Why withhold the nourishment and security that we can give through the simple expression of our commitment?

Some will say, "Well, words are cheap" or "It's no good to talk the talk if you don't walk the walk," and they are right. But the point is that our words and our talk can remind us to walk like we talk and to live like we commit. Finding frequent ways to express our commitments is what keeps us from gradually forgetting or straying from those commitments.

❧

REMEMBER THE GEESE.
BE CONSCIOUS OF COMMITMENT.
HOLD YOUR PRIORITIES IN V FORMATION
WITH FAMILY AT THE FRONT.
ALWAYS COME HOME!

❧

2

The Nature of PRAISE

Crabs are remarkab'e little creatures. Unlike their lobster and shrimp relatives, crabs can run sideways at a fast clip and can burrow quickly into the sand when danger approaches. Like all arthropods, they have to shed their hard shells (exoskeletons) frequently in order to grow. Very young crabs, with a lot of growing to do, get rid of their old shells every three or four days.

I (Richard) was born in Baltimore, and while I don't have much actual memory of those earliest years, I still love hearing my mother tell stories of going "crabbing" on the Maryland shore. Apparently it's fairly difficult to catch the speedy, burrowing little guys, but remarkably easy to keep track of them once they are caught because of their instinct to "pull one another down." Once you have at least two crabs, you just put them in a shallow pan or bucket. A single crab can easily climb out, but if there's another crab there, he will reach up with his claw and pull the first crab back down before he can get up over the edge. Thus you can fill up a bucket with crabs, and though they all try to escape, not a single one will get out because instead of boosting one another up, they follow their strong instinct to pull back anyone who tries to climb above them.

Unfortunately, crablike behavior and habits are also common within our own species. It seems to be a part of human nature to envy those who rise above us and to pull them down literally or verbally or at least within our own critical and judgmental minds. Even within our families we are not exempt. As parents, we often fall into the notion that parenting is all about correcting and criticizing, about punishing and pulling down. We behave as though we think of our job as keeping children in line rather than helping them expand and grow. Our children also do a close imitation of crabs, which we call "sibling rivalry."

Even though parents want the best for their children, they sometimes feel instincts of resentment and resistance when a child wants to move up "over the edge" or is attracted to lifestyles or circumstances beyond what the parents have been able to obtain. Conversely, kids sometimes resent, criticize, and pull down their own parents when they feel they can't meet their expectations or reach the level their parents achieved.

 The Law of the Crabs is doing the opposite of what the crabs do: support and positive affirmation—lifting up instead of pulling down, praise rather than criticism.

One principle that almost all parents *know* (but that hardly any parents *do)* is that since children crave attention, we should give more attention to positive behavior than to negative acting out. Stand in a busy mall sometime and watch parents and children walk by. Who's getting all the recognition and focus? The kids who are behaving themselves are getting ignored. The ones who are crying or complaining or fighting with one another are getting all of their parents' attention.

It's a hard pattern to change, but it's worth the effort because the simple fact is that, over time, praise works and criticism doesn't.

❖ ❖

U n l i k e   the crabs, we must learn that boosting up is the answer, not pulling down.

U n l i k e   the crabs, we must support rather than compete with one another within our families.

U n l i k e   the crabs, we must look for ways to build our children's self-confidence through frequent praise rather than undermining it through constant criticism.

U n l i k e   the crabs, we must truly want our children to rise above and beyond ourselves.

U n l i k e   the crabs, we must praise effort and reward honest attempts.

U n l i k e   the crabs, we must stop trying to catch our children doing something wrong and start trying to catch them doing something right.

U n l i k e   the crabs, we must love our children more than ourselves and make their well-being more important than our own.

L i k e   the crabs, we must learn to shed our old hard shells of judgmental criticism so our softer, more nourishing inner selves can grow.

One day, while we were living in Japan, we saw a simple, memorable example of "doing it right." (Asian cultures are better than ours at recognizing the positive and ignoring the negative.)

We were chatting with Kaiko, a neighbor of ours, in her kitchen, when her little boy came in and began to pester her, tugging at her skirt, interrupting our conversation, whining and being obnoxious. Kaiko completely ignored him. Finally, when he got too loud to ignore, she matter-of-factly (and without even looking at him) scooped him up, opened the nearest door, set him on the other side, and closed it. It happened to be a closet. She continued her conversation with us all the while, as though nothing had happened. A couple of minutes later the closet door opened and the little boy came quietly out and stood politely by his mother. When there was a pause in our conversation, he said, "Excuse me, Mother." Now Kaiko gave him her full attention, listening to his need—which happened to be that he was thirsty—and gave him a glass of water along with an affectionate pat on the head and then a little hug.

It seemed so simple. It worked so well. She had recognized and rewarded the positive and ignored the negative. She had lifted up rather than put down. She had "caught him doing something right."

A mother told us of an experience with her four-year-old, Josh. He had been at a play group earlier in the day where he was the only one who couldn't climb to the top of the monkey bars, so he was feeling a little discouraged and "unconfident." On impulse, Mom lifted him up on her knee and started telling him the things she could think of that he was good at. "You're good at throwing a ball," she said. "You're good at making your bed, and you're really good at making the baby happy when she cries."

By the fourth or fifth compliment, she noticed that Josh was smiling, but now he looked around, apparently trying to find something. "What do you want?" she asked.

"A pen," he said, "I want a pen." She pulled one out of her purse, and he said, "Write those things down—those things that I'm good at."

"Where shall I write them?" she asked, glancing around for a piece of paper.

"Here," Josh said, thrusting out his hand. "Write them right here on my hand; write one on each finger."

So she did. And she said her little Josh, though not even old enough to read them, wouldn't wash his hand for two days.

A father had been learning about "deep affirmations" in a seminar at his work and decided to try the technique on his grown daughter who lived away from home and was currently under a lot of stress. He called, got her answering machine, and just spontaneously left a long message filled with his love for her and his confidence that she would make it through the tough period she was in. He expressed his faith in her, recalling various times when she had met challenges and reached her goals. He told her how much she'd grown as a result of those previous difficult times and assured her that this one would be no different. He invited her to call him back and tell him the latest on her situation, and he promised he would just listen. He told her she was the best daughter anyone could have and reminded her again of how much he loved her and believed in her.

A few weeks later, when they were together, the daughter hugged her dad and whispered to him that she had saved that phone message and listened to it again and again, especially when she felt the lowest. It had given her the strength, the confidence, and the *boost* she needed.

Learn the message of the crabs. Almost any interpersonal problem you may be having with a child can be improved with honest praise. Almost like a magic potion, it softens hearts and helps each individual see the strengths of others. Use the profound psychological power a parent has to lift your children up to the best and happiest people they can be.

It's not easy to change our habits and patterns—to boost rather than pull down, to praise rather than to prod, to give attention to positive behavior rather than negative—but take heart by remembering a positive quality about those same crabs we've been using as a negative example. They shed their hard shells in order to grow! As parents, we can shed our hard shells of criticism and grow a new persona of praise!

❖ ❖

One mother, realizing she was prone to criticism and constant correction of her eight-year-old son, but who sincerely felt that the boy needed every word of it, decided to adopt the "sandwich method." This simply meant putting a slice of praise or positive reinforcement on both sides of the criticism or correction. If she had to say, "Your room still isn't clean," she'd first say something like, "Thanks for putting your plate in the dishwasher after dinner." Then, after the reminder to clean his room, she'd say, "You know, you really are very good at cleaning up when you try."

One dad, in an effort to improve on his largely negative approach to parenting, simply offered his kids a dollar for every time they caught him saying "No." He felt that each "No" was a little pull-down for his children. As he consciously tried to avoid the N-word, he found he could always substitute something like, "It might be better if . . ."

One family started a Sunday dinnertime tradition where they would go around the table and each tell one positive thing they had admired or appreciated about a family member during the previous week.

One father came home one evening and found his five-year-old daughter in his bathroom, where she had filled up his bathtub and put so much soap in it that bubbles and suds were running over onto the floor. It looked like she'd done it innocently, so he resisted his "pull-down" instinct and just sat down for a minute, trying to think of a "boost-up" instead. He forced a smile and said, "Hey, you were trying to clean my tub for me, huh?" Relieved, the little girl ran over and jumped into his arms, confessing, "Yeah, but Daddy, I used way too much soap, didn't I!"

One mom, worried about all the sibling rivalry, fighting, and "pull-down" insults going on between their three young children, was getting exhausted trying to be the judge and jury in every dispute—trying to figure out who did what, who should go to time-out, and so on. One day she realized that the goal was not to blame or punish someone but to help the kids learn to settle their own disputes and to take responsibility for their own actions. She decided to set up a "repenting bench"—a little wooden bench where any two kids who were fighting or arguing had to go and sit side by side. The only way a child could get off the bench was to think of what he did wrong (not what the other child did), then apologize, take back any insults, and give the other child a little hug.

She said it took a little while to establish the policy. She had to teach them the principle of "it takes two to tangle." And even then, the kids usually couldn't imagine what they had done—they sometimes had to ask the child they were sitting on the bench with. But over time they learned what it took to "get off the bench," and began to acknowledge, to apologize, and to resolve. They also learned that it was pointless to blame one another and pull one another down.

One mom with two kids away at college got in the habit of sending each an "affirmation e-mail" once a week. This was different and separate from the regular, newsy e-mails. It consisted simply and only of a complimenting "boost" and an expression of confidence, usually with a reference to one particular quality that she admired and to a memory of a specific time when she had noticed and appreciated that quality.

One family felt they needed a formal way to put more emphasis on complimenting one another. The dad went down to a sports awards shop and bought a simple trophy with a plaque inscribed, "Best intrafamily compliment of the week." At Sunday dinner they instigated a little regular discussion of the compliments anyone in the family had given. The trophy went to (and stayed for the week in the room of) the family member who had given the best—most thoughtful, most honest—*compliment* to another family member during the week.

One grandmother, who tended her two young grandchildren in the afternoons after their day care and before their single mom got home, felt concerned about how tired and negative her daughter was when she came in each evening, and how the fatigue and frustration came out in the form of constant criticism of the children.

This particular grandmother, understanding the pressure and stress her daughter was under, decided the most nurturing thing she could do was to try to help her daughter be more positive and help the children feel more valued. She set the goal of noticing one specific praiseworthy action or behavior each day in each of the children. Instead of telling them to the children, she wrote these down and left them on the counter for her daughter to find later in the evening. Eventually it became a ritual. Grandmother reported each day and began to take delight in praising the children accordingly. The older of the two kids, who was learning to read, began to ask for the notes about herself and to save them in her drawer.

One family had a clipboard by the front door with a sheet that said, "Hardest thing for me today." Kids would write, "Geometry test—third period, 10:30 a.m." or "Play tryout after school." A parent might write, "Presentation to vice president, 3 p.m." The idea was for other family members to be aware and supportive during one another's "pressure points" . . . to think about them at those particular times of the day and perhaps say a little prayer in their behalf.

Our family

_____

_____

_____

_____

_____

What We Learn from the Crabs

❖

Crabs have an instinct to pull one another down
rather than boost one another up.
This reactionary tendency prevents any crab
from climbing very high.
In our family, when we criticize
and put one another down,
we're being like the crabs.
Let's remember to boost one another up
and give one another compliments and praise.
Let's remind one another and always
try to remember not to be like the crabs.

Once again, *how* you give "boosts" instead of "pull-downs"
isn't as important as that you *do* it and stay conscious of it.

In a way, the Law of the Crabs is a natural progression from
the Law of the Geese. First we make sure family members are
constantly and generally aware of our love and commitment,
and then we look for specific, positive ways to show that love by
giving boosts and compliments and affirmations.

The Law of the Crabs is extremely simple, but not easy to
live by. Much of our parental instinct is to criticize, correct,
condemn, and chastise, and no matter how "constructive" we

try to be about it, it almost always has a "pull-down" effect or result. But with conscious effort and practice we can overcome our crablike tendencies and give our children the frequent boosts of support and confidence that will enable and empower them to climb to their full potential.

❖

REMEMBER THE CRABS.
BE AS UNLIKE THEM AS YOU CAN.
RESIST THE INSTINCT TO CRITICIZE.
CULTIVATE THE INSTINCT TO PRAISE.
SHED YOUR SHELL AND GROW.

❖

3

The Nature of
COMMUNICATION

One year, partly because of our teenage son Noah's interest in marine biology and partly because of where we happened to be traveling and lecturing at the time, the whole Eyre family seemed to get immersed in and fascinated with humpback whales. Our first encounter was while we were scuba diving at Molokini Island off the coast of Maui. I (Richard) was with two of our sons (including Noah), and we were about 60 feet down, just minding our own business, watching schools of brightly colored reef fish. Suddenly we heard (and felt) the mysterious pulsing, echoing, squeaking, vibrating, harmonizing song of the humpbacks. It was impossible to tell where they were or how many there were or how close they were, but their song—and their presence— was truly awesome.

I looked into Noah's face mask to see if he was fright- ened, and saw instead a wide-eyed expression of wonder and

The

L
A
W

of the

W
H
A
L
E
S

excitement. We stayed down as long as our air supply would allow, just listening and feeling strangely moved by the songs. There was an honesty and an earnestness and a powerful beauty in the whales' sound. They were very loud at times and seemed to have infinite variety, not only of pitch, but of the emotion or mood they carried. The whole experience lasted only 15 or 20 minutes, but none of us will ever forget it. There was real communication going on there—a communication that carried all kinds of feelings.

In the summer of that same year, we found ourselves on a cruise ship in Alaska where we were presenting a lecture. One day, as we stood on deck watching the blue ice of a glacier sheer off and plunge into the sea, someone on the other side of the deck yelled, "Whale!" The captain cut his engines and we sat still in the water and waited. Even those who had watched whales for years said they'd never seen such a show as we got that day. Five or six huge humpbacks began to surface roll and breach and play within a few hundred feet of the deck where we stood. The still surface would explode as one of the 50-foot-long, 50-ton giants would fly up from the depths and twirl entirely out of the water before smashing back with a splash that sent rolling waves that rocked our massive ship. Noah ran down to a lower deck to be as close as possible, and he actually got soaked from the splash of the closest breach.

The on-board biologist told us later that there were lots of theories about why humpbacks jump and breach. Some think it removes crusted barnacles from their sleek sides. But the most accepted theory is the simplest one: They do it because it's fun. They do it to play and to show off to one another. The ship was equipped with an underwater microphone, so we could hear their songs, which, during this kind of play, were loud and excited and almost constant. They seem to be applauding and approving of one another's underwater and above-water acrobatics.

Individual humpbacks are easy to identify because they each have a completely individual and unique white and black pattern on their fluke—the huge, flat, perpendicular-to-their-body tail that they flip up and flop over as they surface through a breathing roll. With their fingerprint flukes to identify them, biologists have determined how loyal and committed they are to their own "pod," or family, and how most of their extensive communication is between family members.

Their communication allows the whales to engage in remarkable teamwork—a sort of whale-synergy that seems to produce a kind of social enjoyment as well as the practical benefit of gathering food. Two humpbacks from the same family frequently swim down through the water in a synchronized spiral, blowing constantly from their blowholes, to create a cylinder of bubbles called a bubble net. Small fish and plankton stay inside the bubble barricade as the two whales turn and swim up faster than their bubbles rise—up through the bubble cylinder, huge mouths wide open, eating all the fish entrapped there. The efficiency of this "bubble net" technique is one of the *things that enables a mature humpback to eat one and a half tons of food per day.*

The gentlest, most tender, and touching humpback song seems to be the one mothers sing to guide and encourage their baby calves. Humpback babies are born far below the surface, and the first challenge of the new mother is to lift and nudge her new child (with her nose) to the surface, where it can draw its first breath of air. Those who have witnessed this nurturing act say they will never forget the mother's song that goes with it—a song of love and pride and confidence.

There is a wide variety of opinions about these massive animals, and particularly about their wondrous songs. We read a lot of theories and educated guesses and came up with a few of our own. We discovered that humpback whales can communicate with one another through hundreds of miles of ocean, and that family pods stay in virtually constant communication—always knowing one another's whereabouts and status. We read opinions that the songs are most intense and continuous when one family member is hurt or in some form of stress or danger. We discovered that some biologists believe many of their songs serve the purpose of encouraging one another and of giving younger whales constant reassurance of security and a sense of identity and bonding with their own pod. And we deduced that generally only one whale sings at a time. The others listen and respond only when the first is finished. If another pod member sings at the same time, it seems to take the form of harmony, and of agreement and encouragement.

 So what is the Law of the Whales? It is, of course, the lesson of constant, open, and emotionally honest communication. Real and committed family communication avoids many potential problems and holds the key to solving and resolving the problems that do exist. Positive communication in a family is like an open gate that *allows* values to be taught, joy to be shared, and problems to be dealt with. When the gate is closed, pressure builds and individuals become isolated.

❖ ❖

L i k e the whales, our families must strive to communicate almost constantly. The channels need to be always open so teamwork and cooperation can flourish.

L i k e the whales, much of that communication needs to be about approving and encouraging and confidence-giving.

L i k e the whales, the communication needs to be particularly intense and constant in times of stress, danger, or difficulty.

L i k e the whales, we should listen to one another rather than interrupting.

L i k e the whales, our communication needs to involve loyalty and teamwork, building trust and creating real family synergy.

L i k e the whales, our communication has to be tailored for the individual. Each child is as completely unique as a humpback's fluke. One child may need stern, disciplining communication, while another needs a far softer approach.

L i k e the whales, we need to make our communication not a lecture but a song—a song of honest interchange and mutual respect.

Angela was sitting in a therapist's office with her sullen, obviously distraught, fourteen-year-old daughter. "I know what is best for my daughter, and she is not going to be dating until she gets her grades up," she told the therapist. "Boys are just a distraction. She needs to get her homework done, and she needs to practice the piano at least two hours a day. All she wants to do is sit around and watch TV and be with her friends all the time. I know she doesn't agree, but I've been there, and as an adult, I know more than she does right now."

The wise therapist observed the stern, rigid look on the mother's face and the forlorn, hopeless face of the daughter sitting next to her. "Your principles are absolutely correct," he said, "but I worry about how your daughter views your motives and conclusions, which you feel are based on her own best . . ."

Interrupting, and without looking, the mother said, "I know what she thinks, but she's wrong! Doing what she should is much more important than doing what she wants. She just doesn't understand that what she does right now will affect her for the rest of her life."

The therapist smiled at the unrepentant mother and let her have it: "Angela, I'm concerned that you may be setting yourself up for rebellion and failure! If you undermine your communication with your daughter by refusing to really listen to how she feels, your relationship is going nowhere. Until the goals for your daughter's life are hers and not yours, you'll be her adversary rather than her advocate. There's a wall between you right now, and only some deep listening can tear it down."

Startled, Angela heard a ring of truth in what had just been said. She looked at her daughter, who had tears streaming down her face. She'd heard exactly what she had so much wanted to communicate to her mother but had never been given the chance. The mother felt her daughter's heart, and her own heart softened. Something about the look on her child's face had made Angela realize that what her daughter really needed was a mother, not a judge . . . an adviser and a listener, not a dictator. Her daughter needed someone who trusted her and believed in her ability to set her *own* goals and figure out her own future.

In the days that followed, Angela started listening more and lecturing less. She racked her brain for ideas to knock down the great wall she had built so she could begin communicating with her daughter again. She began asking questions about what her daughter wanted to talk about—about her opinions and her hopes, her dreams and goals. Gradually her daughter began to open up. Because she was very artistic, Angela suggested that she make a colorful chart to show her one-year goals in academic, social, and family areas.

It wasn't an overnight process, but before long the daughter's goals were actually more progressive than the goals Angela had tried to set for her with an iron hand and through angry resistance. Angela sensed how completely the dynamic had changed. The initiative had shifted. Now she could be perceived not as a pushy "manager," but as a welcomed consultant. She could ask, "What can I do to help you with your goals?" And she loved the look of determination and pride on her daughter's face when she talked about *her* goals, *her* hopes, *her* plans, *her* dreams.

*S*tan had just about given up in his efforts to communicate with his fourteen-year-old daughter. She was an outstanding young girl—an exceptional student, active in music and sports, and completely swept up in the social life of her first year of high school. But she wouldn't give him the time of day. She acted embarrassed about Stan's blue-collar job and their small apartment, and she was rude and sarcastic with him, impatient with his questions, unwilling to tell him much of anything about her life or her feelings. His questions about school or friends or activities were met with blunt impatient brush-offs like "Fine" or "Good" or "Don't worry about it."

For a while Stan assumed that it was a stage that would pass. But one day he realized that the pattern had been going on for years, and that they didn't have very many more years before she'd be leaving home—hopefully to go to college. He decided he'd better prioritize and try to do whatever it would take to have the kind of relationship with his daughter that he wanted—that he hoped they both wanted.

Once he'd committed himself to the goal of better communication, it didn't seem quite as impossible as it had before. He tried to think of ideas, and when he got one, he'd try it. He found that his daughter responded to written notes, so he wrote little letters of praise and appreciation whenever he noticed or heard about something that made him proud of her. And he found time to drive her to a couple of her music lessons or soccer games each week. He discovered that she liked a particular restaurant and couldn't resist going there for lunch with him on a Saturday. When they were one-on-one in the car or at lunch, she treated his questions less like an interrogation and began giving him some fairly informative answers. She even asked a question or two of her own.

Encouraged, Stan arranged for her to take a ride with him after school one day in the earthmover he operated at the construction site. She seemed impressed. Driving home that evening, at a moment when it felt right, he told her how much he loved her, that he just had to know what she was doing and thinking and feeling, and that he would always try to understand. Stan sensed that there was a breakthrough then—as if his daughter realized he wasn't going to give up, so *she* might as well give in and start talking to him like a real person. She told him a couple of things she was worried about, and to her surprise, he listened rather than judged.

Over the next few weeks, things gradually got better between them. They both felt the trust level improving. The natural, protecting, tender daddy-daughter love began to reassert itself, and while there was still a long way to go, Stan felt they'd turned a corner.

Some close friends of ours had a son, Brady, who was born with severe and debilitating physical handicaps. Doctors said he'd never be able to attend school, and they predicted that Brady would not live beyond eight or nine years old. In a wheelchair he could operate with one finger—the only part of his body that he could control—and with oxygen connected to his weak lungs, this courageous boy outlived all the predictions and graduated from high school. Along the way, Brady gained so many friends that when his feeble strength finally faded and he died at the age of twenty-two, his funeral had to be held in a cavernous music hall theater.

As we sat listening to the eulogies of friend after friend, it occurred to us that they were all saying essentially the same thing. They each thought they were Brady's best friend. Each of them had loved visiting him at his house, even though all Brady could do was lie there and listen, only using his weak and somewhat garbled voice to say, "That's cool," or to ask them another question about themselves.

One peer said: "When you were with Brady, he was with you! He was totally interested in everything you said. It was like you were the most important person in the world. He listened with all of his attention. It was almost like he was saying, 'Well, I don't have a life, but never mind, I'll just live yours with you.'"

The bottom line was that everyone loved Brady because he listened. People wanted to be around him because his interest made them feel worthwhile and important. We're not sure exactly where or how he learned it so well, but Brady knew (and lived) the Law of the Whales.

The bottom line is this: Listening is the key to communication, and without open lines of communication, without the Law of the Whales, a family will never become the learning, growing, trusting place it was intended to be. So parents should insist on it. Do whatever it takes to establish it, to restore it, to maintain it. Discuss the Law of the Whales together. Ask one another where your family's communication is breaking down and why.

❖ ❖

One mom realized that the only two times she seemed to get in a conversation with her thirteen-year-old daughter was on a long drive or very late at night. Instead of bemoaning the fact that those were her only two options and that neither was convenient, she started doing more of both. She'd offer to drive her daughter over to see a friend who'd moved to the suburbs 45 minutes away on the other side of town. And sometimes she'd actually take her daughter to a late movie on a weekend, just to have the late-night communication that seemed to only happen after midnight. "Whatever it takes" was her attitude.

One divorced dad who only got to see his two children every second weekend had been filling his allotted days so full of activities that he realized there usually wasn't much time for communication. He backed off a little and tried to spend more time eating or driving together with his children, or going to quieter, slower-paced places like parks or zoos, which lent themselves to more conversation. He also found that working or doing projects with his kids—from fixing something on the car to building a new doghouse together—seemed to prompt free and spontaneous communication.

One family simply decided to eliminate television. They got rid of all three of their sets, and after a painful and complaining adjustment period, family members began to communicate more. Another family went partway—unplugging TV on weeknights to make more time for homework as well as conversation. Still another family just allowed one hour of watching (or video games or Internet use) per night.

One dad, though he spent a lot of time with his nine-year-old daughter, felt like their communication rarely got past the surface. They talked about school and activities, but they rarely talked about feelings. To try to change that, he consciously began using the word "feel" more frequently, both in his comments and his questions. He would tell her how he felt about things and ask her: "How do you feel about that?"

He also tried to tuck his daughter into bed at night more often, and before leaving the room, he'd ask her to tell him of her "happy" for the day and also of her "sad." This usually helped her open up about her feelings, and he often left these "tucking in" sessions with new insights about his daughter and her day-to-day life.

One mom who had resented the effect "technology" was having on her relationship and communication with her teenage son and daughter—they were always on the computer or playing electronic games—simply decided if she couldn't beat them, she should join them. From her laptop upstairs, she would often e-mail or instant message her kids downstairs in the rec room on the family computer. She also got each of them a low-cost, local-calls-only cell phone so she could find them when necessary, monitor where they were after school, and be sure they were coming home on time on weekend nights. She even invited herself into their chat rooms periodically and got involved with them in some of their online games.

The kids seemed to gain a new kind of respect for her and rapport with her. She didn't try to become their peer or their buddy or their best friend—she remained their parent, but a more savvy and tuned-in parent. Technology evolved from enemy to aide.

One dad set aside every other Saturday (every two weeks) as "Buddy Morning," and he and his son would go for some one-on-one outing then. Dad might have ideas or make suggestions, but the choice (within reason) of where they would go and what they would do was the boy's. They tried to start fairly early on Saturday so neither of them would feel rushed or pressured, and the father let his son choose their topics of conversation as well as their destination. They even kept a "Buddy Book" in which they would include a memento from each time they were together, like a twig from a hike or a drinking straw from their McDonald's breakfast. Years later the boy could flip through that little book and recall where each item came from and what they had done together that day.

One mother who was trying to teach her nine-year-old how to schedule her time discovered that the process had communications benefits. She got her daughter a simple day timer, and the girl seemed flattered that her mom thought she was old enough to use such an adult-type book. The mom, in turn, was proud of her daughter's efforts to keep track of her schedule in the book, and her pride and approval encouraged the daughter to share what she was writing in the schedule.

Every week, the notes and plans she wrote became the subject of meaningful communication about things that were on the daughter's mind. If she wrote "History Test" with big stars around it on Thursday morning, it became more natural to talk about the test and for her mom to help with it. If she wrote something about meeting a new friend or a problem with an old one, it became easy (and helpful) to ask about friends and relationships. Essentially, the mother found that once her daughter had taken the initiative of writing something down that was important to her, she could compliment her for being a self-starter and communicate with her as a helpful, interested adviser rather than a pushy, controlling "dictator."

Our family

What We Learn from the Whales

❖

Humpback whales, the largest creatures on the earth
and with the largest brains,
sing beautiful underwater songs to one another.
Whale families are called "pods,"
and most of the songs seem to be between
members of a pod.
They use their songs to encourage one another
or to warn one another of danger,
and they often sing while they play together.
The most amazing thing is that they
almost never interrupt.
When one whale is singing,
the others listen!
Let's remember the whales and try to be
more like them in our own family.

No one would deny the importance of good and open communication within a family. Fewer small problems would grow into big ones if there were more communication. Fewer children would feel alone and misunderstood; fewer parents would feel so powerless in understanding or helping their kids; fewer siblings would have relationships based only on rivalry.

Like so many things, communication improves and increases just because we're concentrating on it. Thinking of humpback whales may help you to do so!

❖

REMEMBER THE WHALES.
MODIFY YOUR FAMILY COMMUNICATION
AND MAKE IT INTO A LISTENING,
ENCOURAGING SONG.

❖

The Nature of
CONSISTENCY

We've already acknowledged that "The Tortoise and the Hare" is our favorite Aesop's fable. Almost everyone knows the story, but few know the details, and thus they have a hard time really believing that a slow and plodding turtle could actually beat a quick and nimble rabbit.

Here's our version of the real story:

The race was a long one, very long, and the exact destination wasn't known by either contestant. They were told the general direction of the finish line and instructed to watch for signs and indications along the way. The hare set out fast but kept missing the clues and getting off on long detours. He also frequently lost interest as he noticed various "carrots" near the path and became distracted by the applause of spectators who

admired his sleekness. He was in too much of a rush to make con-
versation or form relationships. He covered a lot of distance every
day and was very tired when he got up each morning.

The tortoise moved slowly and tried to observe everything
along the way. He had the habit of starting early each day and
watching for signs. Even though he just plodded along, his fore-
sight and ability to anticipate and look ahead gave him an inter-
esting quality that he called "the speed of going slow." He had
reliable rules, a set schedule, and a predictable pace. There was a
certain stability about him. Because of his deliberate, easygoing
style, he had time to visit with other animals along the way,
many of whom became his friends and told him of shortcuts or
better roads. Once there was a shortcut through an ocean inlet,
and a family member, a sea tortoise, towed him through.

Others liked to walk along with the tortoise. His slow, steady
pace was restful and agreeable, and it always seemed that he had
plenty of time to talk to anyone who wanted to walk along with
him. He was interested in them. He asked lots of questions of those
who joined him, and he seemed to respect them and their ideas.

Some tried to discourage him, telling him that the hare had
passed by long ago and warning the tortoise that it was too late,
that he'd already lost. He took their comments with a wise,
knowing smile and just kept plodding along.

Now, everyone knows that the turtle won. But what is not
commonly understood is how much fun he had in the process
and how much he enjoyed the race. He was always sure of his

direction, he was content with slow, steady progress, and he loved finding signs and making friends and getting help along the way. The rabbit, on the other hand, was pretty much lost all the time. He looked flashy and stylish but he was always hurrying and was never quite sure exactly where he wanted to go. He was erratic and sometimes just couldn't decide how much the race really mattered to him, or if this was really the best race for him to be in.

If children are the race, oh how they appreciate and reward the steady, patient, consistent parent. The rewards and payoffs aren't always immediate, but over time, over the course of the race, parents who hang in there, who remember the finish-line priority of their children and build a consistent, reliable life for them always win in the end.

Parents with a tortoise attitude—who know the race is long and that progress will be gradual—also tend to develop a calmness and confidence that makes children feel secure. Such parents enjoy the race or the process, and they learn that consistency and predictable steadiness is more important to kids than quick fixes.

Some rabbit parents head off down various routes and get so turned around that they think the career path is more important than the family road. They get in the wrong race and begin to think that the family is there to serve and support the job rather than the other way around. They get caught up in winning the approval of others, and too distracted by the "carrots" of ever bigger houses, cars, titles, clothes, and status.

Tortoise parents, on the other hand, even though they're no less aware of the demands and importance of work and career, still try to judge every path by whether it gets them closer to the finish line of well-adjusted kids and a happy family. They build consistency and reliability into little things like meals together, church together, traditions and outings together, stories and prayers at bedtime. They sometimes find shortcuts, such as family vacations that allow a lot of unhurried "talk time," or one-on-one drives where there is lots of communication and many chances to deepen a relationship.

Tortoise parents don't lack ambition, passion, or spontaneity, and they certainly don't have to be stiff or rigid. In fact, the kind of parents who know the destination and know that it will take a good long time to get there can actually loosen up and enjoy the journey. They gain the old wisdom that knows there will be ups and downs but also knows that as long as they keep moving forward, time is on their side. With certain predictable patterns in place, it actually feels less risky to take a chance or try something new now and then.

The Law of the Tortoise is calm, steady consistency that can wrap children in a warm blanket of peaceful predictability.

No matter how cold or random life gets outside the home, there are certain basic and consistent things they can always count on inside the home: a certain sense of being cared about, some reliable family rituals, a recurring pattern of order and schedule, and a limitless amount of unconditional love.

Such a home is a calmer, safer, more magnetic place than the chaotic and often confusing world our children inhabit at school and in their social environment outside the home. Tortoise parents tend to create a plodding, comfortable place with traditions and with a pace that is purposefully slow enough to allow easy conversation and relaxed listening.

❖ ❖

L i k e   the tortoise, we must get up each day and keep at it, realizing that it is not our speed or brilliance that will get us through, but our consistency, not our *ability* but our *availability*.

L i k e   the tortoise, we need to understand that it's a long race and that there will be lots of little victories and defeats along the way—each of which we can learn from.

L i k e   the tortoise, we should set up schedules and patterns that give order to our homes. We should look for and appreciate the occasional spontaneous shortcut, but we should avoid the big detours that take us off the real road, which leads to the finish line of a strong family.

L i k e   the tortoise, we should never be in too big a hurry to listen, to notice, to share.

L i k e   the tortoise, we should seek advice and help and be flexible enough to change our direction when we see a better way.

L i k e   the tortoise, we should have regular, reliable rituals and timely traditions in which others—particularly our children—can find security and identity.

*B*irthday traditions have always been big at our house. There are certain crazy things we always do as a family on a particular person's birthday. Since my (Richard's) birthday is in October, our first kids, when they were young, insisted on going out and raking up huge piles of autumn leaves and then jumping wildly in them, throwing them at one another, getting buried in them, stuffing them down one another's necks, and anything else they could think of.

I assumed that particular tradition would die out as the kids got older, but all through high school they kept it alive every birthday— now with friends joining in, and changing the venue to the public park where there were enough leaves for a real party!

I finally realized the full power of family traditions one autumn when our oldest three had left home. One was away at college and two were in Eastern Europe doing missionary work and volunteering at orphanages. The day before my birthday, I got three envelopes in the mail. Assuming they were birthday cards, I set them on my desk to open the next day. On my birthday, after doing our leaf-jumping with the younger kids, I picked up the first envelope. As I slit it open, a bright Romanian leaf fell out, with a note from a daughter saying she loved me and that she'd honored our family tradition in a park in Bucharest. The second letter contained more leaves, this time from Bulgaria. The third held a leaf from our son's university campus.

Through my tears I began to understand that the little rituals and traditions we establish in our family are more than fun and games—they are the glue that holds families together, and the source of a connection and an identity that our children never want to lose.

A woman we'll call Joan went to church one Sunday with a heavy heart. She felt that she had completely failed as a parent. Her divorce had affected each of her children in a different way. She hadn't heard from her nineteen-year-old son for three months, and he'd finally called early that morning. But the call was from a county jail in southern California where he was being held for drunk and disorderly conduct. "I wasn't drunk," he protested on the phone, "just a little high." The purpose of the call was to ask her to come and bail him out. She'd gone to church to try to decide what to do and to ask God's forgiveness for her total failure as a parent.

Coincidentally (or was it?) the sermon was about eternity. The pastor spoke about how long life is and how many things time can heal. Then he added that eternity is a lot longer, so consider what can be healed there. "To those who believe in time and in eternity, there is no failure until we give up," he said, "and I promise you, unequivocally, in this God-designed system, that if you never give up you will ultimately succeed as a parent."

Joan spent the rest of her time in the church that Sunday repenting and asking God's forgiveness—but it was not for her "failure" as a parent, it was for giving up. She resolved one simple thing that made her a different woman when she left the church than when she came in: that she would never give up, that she would never, in time or eternity, quit the job of mother. Things were not good, but infinite time was on her side.

Learn the Law of the Tortoise. Keep your mind on the long-range goal of children who become happy and functional adults and of family bonds that grow stronger with time.

❖ ❖

One father noticed how much the tensions and stress he brought home from the office affected his children. It was as though they picked up on his high stress vibrations and became restless and hard to manage just by being around him. He adopted a new pattern of sitting quietly in his car for a few minutes after he'd pulled into the garage and before he went into the house. He relaxed and meditated and consciously tried to disengage himself from any worries or stress from the office.

Then he did one thing more. He visualized walking into a bit of chaos. His wife might be depressed, but he would be receptive, sympathetic, and encouraging. His children might be whining or bickering, but he would be calm and interested in what they'd done that day. It didn't always go just as he'd visualized, but at least he went in calm and prepared and didn't make things worse. "And," he said, "when you imagine and anticipate the worst case scenario, it's not usually that bad, so you feel pretty good."

One blended, multicultural family had been expending a lot of effort to all "get on the same page." The African American father and his two teenage sons had one set of traditions, habits, and even food preferences, and the Hispanic mother and her nine-year-old had a completely separate set. When they first got together, the mom and dad thought the best course was to each pull away from their own culture and melt somewhere in the more generic middle. Then they realized that it was not less family traditions they needed, but more.

Since both parents worked and had about an equal amount of time at home, they set up a system where they would each be the "general household manager" on alternate months. One month, Mom would run the house and the meals according to her tastes and traditions. The dad would participate, but since he wasn't in charge, he would have a little extra time to concentrate on his work and outside interests. The next month they would switch, and Dad would take the lead in running the house. The kids got into it and enjoyed the variety and spirit of the thing. In the process, they each built bridges to a culture other than their own and developed a whole new set of friends and perspectives.

One mother, with a growing realization of the importance and identity offered by family patterns and consistency, wanted to put more emphasis on the traditions and rituals the family already had. She created a "family traditions book" with a little write-up on their rituals—from what they did on each child's birthday and on Christmas to what they did each week at Sunday dinner. In order to get the children involved, she asked her seven- and nine-year-olds to draw a picture to "illustrate" each of the traditions.

One stay-at-home dad who was the primary caregiver for his three children was troubled that he always had too many things on his to-do list—more by far, it seemed, than his working wife. She left him lists of errands on top of all the things the kids needed, and he found himself running from one thing to the next and having little time to just be with his children. (His young son had just complained, "Dad, you're always too busy.") Finally, the father decided he had to make a change. Part of his effort was to post two anonymous quotes on the kitchen wall. One read: "A busy man cannot be wise, and a wise man will not be busy." The other said: "Never choose the urgent over the important."

One couple had been convinced for years that if they could just have dinner each evening with their six-, eight-, and twelve-year-olds, it would provide the closeness and communication they felt they lacked. But if one of them didn't have to work late, the other did. And if by some miracle they both got home on time and picked up the kids from their after-school program, then it was soccer night or piano lessons.

They finally realized that the only times they had any real control over were early morning and late evening. So, they started gathering the kids to read aloud together for five or ten minutes just before the six-year-old's bedtime, and discovered that they could actually make it happen three or four times a week with all three kids and at least one of the parents participating. (The twelve-year-old daughter would come if she could be the reader.) That bit of structure seemed to get everyone to bed a little earlier, so they made a second adjustment. They tried to get everyone up a few minutes earlier in order to have breakfast together. After a few weeks of struggle it actually began happening most mornings, and some of the dinnertime conversation they'd fantasized about began to happen at breakfast time.

One divorced couple with joint custody of their two elementary-age children were told by a school counselor that the dramatically different patterns and expectations at their two homes were having a confusing, disruptive effect on the kids. Since their love for their children was the one thing they could agree and get together on, they met with the children and the counselor and had the kids pick the things they liked best at each house. (Somewhat surprisingly, the children liked the most predictable and structured things that each of their parents did—like Mom's breakfasts promptly at 7 a.m., or Dad's insistence that homework be done right after school.) Mom and Dad agreed on certain things that would happen consistently regardless of which house the kids were in.

One dad, who had a Saturday morning golf ritual with his buddies, was facing increasing pressure from his wife to spend Saturdays with their two young daughters instead. They negotiated and compromised. He started golf earlier and came home by 2:00 for "Daddy time." The girls planned what they wanted to do, and he was at their disposal. As the years passed, "Daddy time" became a permanent fixture and provided the time, the place, and the regularity for him to be consistently involved in his daughters' lives.

One grandfather whose ten-year-old granddaughter had a half-day school schedule on Fridays told the girl's parents that he'd like to pick her up from school at noon on Fridays and care for her until 3:30, when her mother got home from work. The three and a half hours became a golden time for them. They'd go places or work together on one of his carpentry projects. Because her grandfather had no agenda other than being with her, the granddaughter found the time relaxing and felt a nourishing, nurturing calmness that she looked forward to each week.

One single mother decided her biggest inconsistency was her changing expectations with her kids, including the erratic discipline she used with them. If she was in a good mood, they could get away with almost anything, and if she was stressed or uptight, they got yelled at and grounded for almost nothing. Over the course of the next few weeks, she and the children had several "house rules meetings" where they worked out what the ongoing, consistent rules would be and what the punishment would be for breaking each one.

Our family

_____

_____

_____

_____

_____

What We Learn from the Tortoise

❖

The reason the turtle won the long race was that
he was consistent. He got up every day and just kept
plodding, while the rabbit kept getting distracted
and putting other things first instead of
concentrating on the race.
The turtle had certain things he did every day—
certain traditions that kept him going.
Because he wasn't in a hurry, he had time to talk to
people and make friends. Since he knew what
really mattered, he was calm and flexible and relaxed, so
nothing bothered him much.
We can be like turtles in our family by just working
every day to make our family better and love
one another more. We can have family
traditions, habits, and patterns that everyone agrees on
and enjoys. We can try to stay peaceful like the turtle,
and to always have time for one another.
That's how we can win at being a family that lasts.

*P*arents can't plan and predict and program everything, and
those who try to do so end up driving themselves nuts.
Schedules work some of the time, but our kids are as busy and

overscheduled as we are, and even our most cherished traditions sometimes get shoved aside by the needs and circumstances of the moment. But the Law of the Tortoise is that we just keep trying, keep putting family first, keep being there for the kids, keep working at making everything work. In the end, our kids love us not because we always succeed or do everything right. They love us because we never give up on them or on the family we're trying to build. The real reward is for effort!

❖

REMEMBER THE LAW OF THE TORTOISE.
BE A STEADY, DEPENDABLE PARENT.
ESTABLISH THE SCHEDULES, HABITS,
AND TRADITIONS THAT GIVE CHILDREN THE COMFORT
OF CONSISTENCY AND THAT ASSURE
AN EVENTUAL GOOD FINISH IN THE LONG RACE
OF RAISING CHILDREN.

❖

The Nature of DISCIPLINE

There is a zoo less than a mile from our house. In fact, we tell visitors how to find our house by saying, "Go up past the zoo." (When all our kids were still at home, we used to add, "Actually, we're part of the zoo.")

The elephants were always a main attraction for our children and their friends, who seemed endlessly entertained not only by their size, but also by that remarkable and unique arm/nose/hand/drinking straw/trumpet/radar tower combination called a "trunk."

Our own adult fascination with elephants and their trunks didn't start until we were able to observe African elephants at their home, on the Serengeti and Masai Mara in Kenya. There, instead of the slow and clumsy and sleepy creatures in the zoo, they were fast and agile and alert, holding their trunks high to pick up scents, running through the tall grass at 30 miles an hour and changing direction on a dime when something unexpected appeared in their path.

When we were able to approach them slowly and cautiously, from downwind, we got a whole new education—particularly on how parent elephants use those amazing trunks with respect to their baby elephants. The parent's trunk is a gentle shower for baby's bath and a talcum duster to apply the fine African dust afterward. It's a shrill trumpet of warning if the baby is stepping out of line or into danger, and it's a stout rope blocking the baby's passage toward somewhere the parent doesn't want him to go.

With a little research, we later discovered that an elephant's trunk is such a complex and intricate implement that it takes about 50,000 separate muscles to control it. Automation engineers and robotics experts have tried in vain to build a mechanical arm with similar strength and dexterity. The trunk is surprisingly tender and light of touch as the mother elephant caresses and fondles her baby, then remarkably strong as it effortlessly picks up and throws aside a 500-pound log in its baby's path. It's hard to imagine anything in nature that is so strong, so tender, so versatile, and so flexible.

If only our love for our children could have all those same qualities: firmness and flexibility, strength and sensitivity, toughness and tenderness, discipline and discretion, steel and sweetness, restraint and release, intervention and independence.

Love without discipline can be dangerous and damaging. Love that is unintelligently applied, that gives too many things the children haven't earned, can spoil our kids, rob them of their own initiative, and give them false perspectives about how the world works. Picture a family where kids get everything they want—money whenever they ask, more clothes than they need, their own car when they're sixteen, no household responsibilities, no discipline to speak of, parents who bail them out whenever they get into trouble. It's not hard to predict the effects of this kind of "spoiling."

On the other end of the spectrum, parental love that is too demanding and too harsh doesn't feel much like love at all. Parents who try to express their love mostly through unbendingly strict rules and overly demanding expectations can suck the joy and tenderness out of family relationships. Picture a family that is punishment-oriented, kids always being grounded, rules for everything, early and inflexible curfews, children expected to earn every dime of spending money, no help with college even though the parents can afford it. Again, it's easy to predict some of the results of too much "toughness."

The Law of the Elephant's Trunk is the fine balance between "tough love" and "tender love." It's about adopting the best aspects from both ends of the spectrum. Kids do need discipline, schedules, clear expectations, and family responsibilities. But they also need tolerance and tenderness and help with no strings attached.

* *

L i k e   the elephant's trunk, our love needs to caress them and hug them every day.

L i k e   the elephant's trunk, our love has to set clear limits on where they can go and what they can do.

L i k e   the elephant's trunk, our love must shower them with approval and dust them with confidence, but it must also warn them loudly and clearly of danger.

L i k e   the elephant's trunk, our love should remove barriers in their path but let them walk the path under their own power.

L i k e   the elephant's trunk, our love must be versatile and flexible, seeing children's needs and willing to be sometimes tough and sometimes tender.

"Nothing good happens after midnight," one set of concerned and conscientious parents reasoned a few years ago when the first of their three children became a teenager. They preached that "the vast majority of car accidents, excessive drinking, and sexual promiscuity occur after midnight." And as with the first, they told the other children who entered that teenage phase that their curfew had nothing to do with trust and that it was all about safety. They explained that it was the actions of *others* that could endanger them. Not without some grumbling, the kids agreed that at least for the immediate future the stroke of midnight was the magic weekend moment when they should be safely inside the front door.

Yet here it was, the third time in a row that the eldest of the three, fifteen-year-old Scott, had missed his curfew, and he seemed unrepentant and even a little belligerent when his mom questioned him about it. "Why do you care so much?" he asked. "None of my friends have a curfew! Why do you always need to know where I am? Quit being so overprotective. I'm smothered! Let me live my life!"

The excuses Scott offered for breaking a family law were pretty weak. The first time was forgivable. The second time, his parents thought he'd be so embarrassed that he would never let it happen again. But the third time required action.

At 12:40 a.m., Scott's dad began calling the homes of his son's friends, much to even his mom's chagrin, who pictured him waking entire households. Through a network of detective work, phone calls, inconvenienced households or not, Dad discovered where the prodigal son was.

They found Scott playing video games at a friend's house at 1:15 a.m. In his teenage mind he had somehow reasoned that his parents would go to sleep if it was late enough and not notice that he wasn't there. Now, he was mortified to have both his parents pop in and tell him it was time to come home. Initially, back at home, there were bad feelings and harsh words, but his parents insisted on talking until things were worked out—all night, if necessary. Scott finally broke down and told them that he felt controlled unnecessarily and stripped of his free agency. And his mom explained to him exactly how a parent feels, not only when a child is unaccounted for, but also when he's breaking a commitment to his family.

By 3 a.m. all the feelings had been laid out on the table. Though lots of things were said in haste and defense, in the end Scott felt the depth of his parents' concern and understood that his father and mother were not administering boundaries to make his life miserable or because they wanted to have power over him, or even that they wanted to go to sleep instead of worrying about him (although they admitted that was part of it). Their prime motive was that they loved him and wanted him to be safe in every sense of the word. When Scott really got that message, he felt warmed and valued.

Years later, married and with a baby daughter, Scott remembers that night clearly and calls it one of the best things his parents ever did for him. Though he never would have admitted it as a fifteen-year-old, he wanted to be stopped. It proved that his parents really loved him. He even admits that the night he was dragged away from his friends by a mad dad and a worried mom was the beginning of a new relationship. From then on, Scott and his two younger siblings knew that a family law was a family law. He loved knowing that his dad loved him so much that he was willing to do whatever it took to impress upon him the importance of a commitment. He can hardly wait to be the same kind of dad.

*O*ne of the most inspirational things you can see in this world is a parent who, by the sheer force of will, breaks a destructive pattern of behavior that has gone on through many past generations and starts a more positive and respectful parental behavior that will carry forward into future generations.

We have a friend, now a single mother of three, who was physically and verbally abused by both of her parents throughout her childhood, just as they had been abused by theirs. She's a large and somewhat gruff woman, qualities that make her highly effective in her factory supervisory job. Yet with her children, she is an amazing example of tenderness and patience.

This friend told us that her parents' bad example motivated her resolution to be the opposite with her own kids. Many parents have made this kind of vow, only to fall into the same patterns as their parents. This mom, though, went a step further than vowing to be different. She actually took the time to write a careful and thorough *description* of the kind of mom she wanted to be. She didn't include what she didn't want to be or the mistakes her parents had made that she wanted to avoid. She just defined and described, completely from the positive side, the kind of tender, nurturing, calm, and controlled mom she wanted to be. She reads that description, and sometimes adds to or edits it, nearly every week. It has crept into her subconscious and influences how she responds to and treats her children.

*I*n our own family, much of our learning process revolved around elephant trunk trial and error. We once sat down with our first three little children and tried to set up family laws by democratic process. Between the five of us, we nominated and confirmed about 35 laws ranging from "never hit other little girls" to "don't pud in puds" (don't plug in plugs). Needless to say, these "rules" were seldom remembered and erratically enforced.

It took us years to figure out how to simplify. We eventually ended up with just four one-word family laws:

1. Peace
2. Respect
3. Order
4. Asking

The penalties began to be effective only when they were as simple as the laws:

1. Go to time-out together until you apologize to each other.
2. Start over and say it respectfully.
3. If your room gets too messy, you can't leave the house till it's clean.
4. Next time, you can't go.

With regard to curfews, for several years running we had either four or five teenagers in our house, and the main lesson we learned was to balance firmness and flexibility. There were times when kids did have circumstances beyond their control when it came to making their curfew. Important relationships were being discussed, high school dances had after-dance activities that lasted longer than expected, and sometimes cars broke down or rides failed to show up. There were even times when videos weren't finished, and since our child was the "ride," he or she would call and explain that they needed a few more minutes.

When the age of cell phones finally arrived, it became so much easier to keep in touch. Often, a call at the stroke of midnight saying, "I'm going to be just a little late because . . ." was all we needed. We learned that there has to be a "letter of the law" before you can look for the spirit of the law—that the time for firmness and the time for flexibility are pretty obvious when everyone makes the extra effort to love and understand one another.

Not only with curfews, but with all disciplinary decisions with our children, our greatest challenge is remembering (and reminding our children) that toughness and tenderness are both part of the same trunk.

A related note on the irony of life: The only time I (Linda) can ever remember actually falling asleep before one of the kids got in on a weekend was when he and his friends were in a car being chased all over town by kids in a gang with guns. True story. When he arrived home at 2 a.m., having never been so scared in his life, his parents were sleeping like babies.

Learn the Law of the Elephant's Trunk. Understand that love that is too demanding can separate us emotionally from our children just as surely as love that is too indulgent. Find the balance. Realize that children need and respond to both discipline and gentleness, but that too much of either without enough of the other can push them away.

Another beautiful image of free African elephants is the baby's first use of his own trunk—to reach up and hold the tail of his mother so he can follow in her footsteps. Children learn to use their "trunks" by the example of ours. If we want a child to grow into an adult possessing both strength and sensitivity, then we must be sure that our example, particularly in how we treat that child, has the right balance of firmness and tenderness.

The two aren't like the opposite positions of a toggle switch. We don't have to constantly choose between them and turn off the tenderness whenever we turn on the toughness. They actually enhance each other and can blend like searing hot and biting cold combining into a comfortable warmth. Our toughness can be tender as we explain why a rule must be obeyed or a responsibility must be met. And our tenderness can be tough when we say, "That's enough," and expect an adequately comforted child to get over it and move on. It's the firmness that allows us to be tender without spoiling children, and it's the tenderness that allows us to be correctly disciplined and demanding without discouraging them.

❖ ❖

One mom, as her two little twins grew into toddlerhood, realized how different the needs of different children can be when it comes to discipline. One of the boys, extremely sensitive and tenderhearted, didn't need—and couldn't handle—anything beyond a stern look from her. The other twin, more aggressive and stubborn, didn't respond at all until he was firmly sent to time-out.

The mom resolved to try always to see them as individuals rather than as a matched pair and, while trying to be consistent, to nevertheless tailor her discipline to their natures and personalities.

One couple with three elementary-school-age children decided to ask them what they thought the punishments should be for various infractions—from hurting one another to not putting their clothes away to not asking permission before they went somewhere. Surprisingly, the kids came up with more severe punishments than the parents would have: "grounded for a week," "no allowance," even "put us in our room for a week with only bread and water." The parents worked out more moderate penalties *with* the kids and then felt more empowered to enforce their family rules.

One single mother read a study about the fact that most children who lose all contact with and become completely estranged from their parents come from one of two types of parents:

1. The "whatever" type who let their kids have whatever they want and don't really know or care what it is ("Do whatever you want, I'll be out anyway").

2. The "overly demanding" type ("I don't care what your friend's problem is, you're not leaving this house until your room is clean and your homework is done").

In thinking about it, this mom realized that she was dangerously close to the second kind of extreme. She was trying to be both parents by being overly restrictive. The thought occurred to her that a clean room really isn't as important as helping a friend with a problem—that "Tell me how you feel about this and then I'll tell you how I feel" makes more sense than saying, "You're grounded." She went so far as to decide that sometimes "Dishes can wait while you have fun" could be an acceptable policy.

One dad caught his small daughter in a bit of mischief, which was not that unusual, but in his anger, and as she looked up at him, he noticed a flicker of fear in her eyes. Distressed that she would feel afraid of him, he made a conscious effort over the next few weeks to work on the tenderness side of the relationship. He started giving her more hugs, and whenever he tucked her in bed he gave her the choice between two different "snugs": "Do you want the princess snug or the bouncy snug?" Though the names were different every night, all snugs involved a cuddling kind of elaborate tuck-in that left his daughter giggling and warm. The dad found that these "tender times" changed the way he thought about his daughter and decreased the number of times he felt angry or upset at her.

One single mom kept trying to get her strong-willed seven-year-old son to obey her, as the child seemed to become more and more defiant. She finally realized that as the only two members of the family, they were having a classic power struggle—a battle of wills that neither would win. She concluded that the principle she wanted to teach her son was not submissive obedience to *her*, but obedience to *law*.

Over the next few weeks, she talked to the boy about laws and why they were important: traffic laws, criminal laws, and so on. When she felt the time was right, she brought up the concept of family laws: "If we have traffic laws to keep us safe and to help everything work better, do you think we could think together of some family laws that might do the same thing?" Once they had developed and agreed on a few simple, basic rules, and a consequence to go with breaking each one, there was a subtle psychological change. It wasn't about power or who was biggest or strongest or who had to obey whom. It was about the laws they had agreed on, laws they had developed together for the mutual good.

One couple couldn't seem to come together on their tenderness-toughness balance. The mom might have boiled her philosophy down to "tender trust" and the dad to "demanding discipline." The dad thought the mom was way too permissive and laid-back with the kids, and the mom, of course, thought the dad was much too strict and firm. She was all about love and leniency. He was all about rules and responsibility. One day they went to look at puppies. (Mom thought the kids ought to have one; Dad said only if there were rules.) They went to a kennel that had a great reputation for dogs that were well-trained and well-mannered yet were also very playful and fun. Impressed with the dogs they found there, Mom and Dad asked the kennel owner how he achieved that balance of qualities. Easy, the owner said. "Have a high fence but have a lot of space and a lot of freedom and a lot of fun *within* that fence."

The parents came to think of that kennel as a metaphor for the kind of home they wanted to have, one that incorporated *both* the fences of the firm rules and clear boundaries the dad was so inclined toward *and* the freedom and flexibility the mom wanted the kids to have.

One family had a long talk about the word "Why" during a road trip they took together. Dad's opinion was that kids shouldn't be allowed to ask why because it just went on and on; whatever answer he gave, they just said "Why?" to that answer too. The kids pointed out that people should have a reason for things—even parents—and that kids ought to have the right to know what it was. They finally agreed that kids would be allowed to ask why *once*, and that Mom or Dad would try to give a *real* answer, and that was it.

One rather traditional and conservative family had a scriptural saying framed and mounted on their wall: "Reproving at times with sharpness, but afterward showing an abundance of love lest he esteem thee to be his enemy." They thought it applied particularly to parent-child relationships and that it reminded them to be sure their discipline or correction never created doubts in their kids' minds about their love for them.

Its effect and application was illustrated one night when a son made a sarcastic, insulting remark to his mother, and the dad intervened immediately and rather harshly. He grabbed the boy firmly by the shoulders, made him look straight in his eyes, and said, "You will *never* talk to my wife like that!"

The boy, who was probably about ten or eleven, had tears start to well up in his eyes, and his chin began to quiver. "Sorry," he mumbled.

The dad, still firm and still demanding eye contact, said, "It's your mom who needs an apology, not me."

The boy did apologize to his mom, and his father, following the scriptural advice on the wall, pulled him into a deep hug and said, "Okay, son. I know you love your mom. And you know I love my wife, and I love *you* too much to ever let you talk to her that way."

He held that hug for quite a while—longer than the arm's-length shoulder grab—and the mom came over and got in on the hug, too. She said, "I love you son, and I know you love me. I'll bet when you're a dad you'll be sure your kids respect your wife too."

One grandmother was left to raise a ten-year-old boy when his full-custody father was killed in an auto accident. She soon realized that the boy's biggest problem, apart from having lost his dad, was that he'd been given everything he wanted. The father hadn't had much time for the boy and had tried to make up for it with presents and by indulging his son in whatever he wanted to do. The grandmother's challenge was to apply tenderness and sympathy as she and the boy shared their grief in the loss of his father, but then to also try to teach the boy the self-discipline and self-reliance that he had not yet learned.

As she got to know her grandson, she realized how bright and conceptual he was and that he was at an age where he could understand both of his two needs. They talked openly about their grief and the way they could help each other through it. They also talked about their new life together and the responsibilities the boy would be expected to assume. He appreciated her honesty, and the balance between tenderness and toughness began to work for both of them.

One family learned the tenderness-toughness lessons from their grandparents. The wife's mother was the epitome of firmness. When the grandkids were at her house, she made it very clear what the rules were and that she expected them to be obeyed. Yet within that firm framework, she was loving and tender to her cherished grandkids. The husband's father, on the other hand, seemed to start from the tenderness side. He loved to hold the kids, tell them stories, whisper them secrets, clip their tiny fingernails and toenails, but within that atmosphere of tenderness, he was firm in correcting them when they needed it.

It was as though one was saying, "I'm firm and that allows me to be flexible," while the other was saying, "I'm flexible and that allows me to be firm." The husband and wife concluded that you could start with your predominant nature, whether tough or tender, and then add the other quality to it to create the balance.

Our family

> ### *What We Learn from the Elephant's Trunk*
> ❖
>
> A mother elephant's trunk is so tender that she uses it to pat her babies, to give them showers, to carefully flick away little wasps or horseflies from baby's back. But her trunk is so strong it can move big rocks and logs from the path and can reach out and stop her babies if they're headed into danger. If we really love someone, especially a child, we have to be very tender and understanding, but also very firm about what's right and wrong.
>
> Baby elephants follow their parents' example and learn quickly how to use their trunks very softly and very strongly, too.
>
> In our family, let's try hard to be kind and tender to one another but really tough about keeping our rules and doing what's right.

*T*he bottom line, it seems, is that toughness and tenderness can and should both spring from love. When they do, they're coordinated and complementary. When we openly and honestly show our love for our children through tenderness, it's all good! And when we openly and honestly show our love through toughness, it's all good. The important thing is to *connect* both sides clearly and obviously to each other and to connect both to genuine and unconditional love.

❖

REMEMBER THE LAW OF THE ELEPHANT'S TRUNK.
TELL CHILDREN HOW MUCH YOU LOVE THEM
AND EXPLAIN THAT IT'S BECAUSE OF
THAT LOVE THAT YOU HAVE
TO BE SURE THEY DO WHAT'S RIGHT,
THAT THEY FOLLOW RULES,
AND THAT THEY ARE SAFE.

❖

The Nature of
SECURITY

Walking into a forest of Sequoia redwoods is like entering a cathedral. The massive overhead boughs filter the sunlight like stained glass, and the size and straightness of the rough red towering trunks inspires an awe and reverence that makes you want to move slowly and softly.

Our oldest daughter and her husband and two little boys live in northern California and love to hike in the redwood groves that are within easy driving distance from their home. Whenever we go there to visit our grandkids (and their parents), the redwoods with their majesty and serenity are always on the short list of places they want to take us.

Before we had that personal connection, if someone said "redwood," we most likely would have thought first of a porch or a deck—constructed of redwood because of the unique properties of that wood, which don't allow it to warp or rot. Nowadays, though, when someone says "redwood," we think of being among those massive trees with our grandchildren. The giant Sequoia redwoods are truly huge—the tallest members of nature's kingdom, reaching over 300 feet straight up—a football field on its end, and thick enough to accommodate a drive-through tunnel in their trunk. You thought the humpback whale was big at 50 tons? A full-grown redwood weighs 40 times as much—over 2000 tons!

But what may actually be more amazing than how big the redwoods are or how tall they stand is how long they stand and the fact that, despite their large, wind-catching limbs and their very shallow roots, they stand firm against the strongest storms and the wildest wind. Their secret is simple: Redwoods grow together in groves and intertwine their shallow roots. Thus, the roots of one tree in the grove are the roots of all the trees, interlaced underground and able to hold each tree upright no matter what kind of gale goes on above.

You don't see crooked redwoods. Lesser trees, even those with more root structure and less mass for the wind to catch, sometimes assume a "wind posture," becoming slanted and crooked to accommodate the prevailing breezes. Redwoods, though, with their interlocking roots, grow straight as well as tall. They are parallel with one another and perpendicular to the ground.

Perhaps the natural resistance of redwood to rot has something to do with the strength, straightness, and longevity of the trees, which in turn is attributable to the way redwoods grow in groves and link their roots.

The Law of the Redwoods is mutual intrafamily support, open expression of love, consistent emotional closeness, and shared moral and successful identity. Families that grow together and stand together, appreciating and intertwining their roots, staying in parallel harmony with one another and at perpendicular odds with base materialism, will reach lofty goals, survive gale-force trials, and be free from the rot of amorality.

We grow in our own family groves simply by staying together and doing things together. We intertwine our roots by supporting one another, by knowing and having contact with extended family and special family friends or godparents, and by having and honoring family rituals and traditions.

It is also very helpful to children if they know something about their genealogical roots—their ancestors—so they can draw strength and identity from those who went before—those who gave us not only our names and personal heritage, but our very genetics. It's hard to know where you're going if you don't know where you've come from. Children who are taught about their ancestral roots have an unseen secondary strength, a beneath-the-surface support and identity system that enhances their self-image and gives them an inner confidence and sense of values and morality that is based on where and who they came from. Everything about our great-grandparents may not be uplifting or honorable, but we can *choose* the stories we tell and the ancestors we focus on.

Adopted children, stepchildren, or children in blended families should be taught that *your* ancestors are now theirs also. When they got you, they also got your whole family tree. These children can actually come to understand that they have the blessing of two "root systems"—yours *and* their own genetic and original culture roots.

We live in a mobile time, a transient society where geographic roots or "being from someplace" seems to matter less than it used to. But our genealogical roots, and knowing enough about our ancestors to link ourselves with them, can give us a sense of stability in an unstable world. Said another way, most people's "place roots" don't go as deep now as they once did. Phrases like "The family's roots were planted deep in the community" wouldn't work with many families today. In light of our transience, our cultural, ancestral, and extended family roots matter more than ever because they serve as a broad intertwining support mechanism and can help a child know who he is morally and spiritually, as well as physically.

❀ ❀ ❀ ❀ ❀ ❀ ❀ ❀ ❀ ❀ ❀ ❀ ❀ ❀ ❀ ❀ ❀ ❀ ❀ ❀

L i k e   the redwoods, we must grow together and grow close to one another.

L i k e   the redwoods, we must embrace one another physically.

L i k e   the redwoods, we must hold tight to one another emotionally and spiritually and link our destinies.

L i k e   the redwoods, we should know our roots, appreciate their strength and interconnections, and understand that we can draw security and identity from them.

L i k e   the redwoods, we should stand tall and straight for our children and pass our common identity on to them with respect and with pride.

L i k e   the redwoods, we should "bloom where we're planted," be grateful for our own heritage and culture rather than wishing for someone else's, and notice the blessings of where our roots are, rather than wanting to move elsewhere.

We lived in England for a time, and because our heritage and genealogy is mostly British and Swedish, we took advantage of our proximity and took excursions to the regions where our ancestors had lived for generations. We had expected it to be an interesting experience, but it was more than that. It was an emotional adventure!

We found the old schoolhouse in rural southern Sweden where our children's great-great-grandfather had been the headmaster. Although it was now converted into someone's summer home, some of the old school desks and the ancient blackboards were still there. Our own children sat in the desks, and we told them stories about the old schoolmaster Swen Swenson, who had taught so many children in that room and who, with his wife Tilda, had summoned enough courage and adventurous spirit to emigrate with their family across the ocean to America. We walked out into the ancient, mossy forest behind the school and looked up at the massive trees, which of course had been smaller when Swen and Tilda walked the same forest paths.

Later that same summer, we went up into Lincolnshire, England, where another great-great-grandfather, James Eyre, had met his sweetheart, Ann, before their own emigration to America. We found family records in an old parish church that showed that James's father was named "Hare" rather than Eyre, and we learned from the old sexton that Lincolnshirites drop their H's, so the illiterate farmers, when reporting their names to the census takers, probably said "Air," which was recorded as "Eyre," as in Jane Eyre. (Incidentally, prior to that discovery, we had thought that our ancestry was through one Sir George Truelove, who, in the Battle of Hastings in 1066, had saved William the Conqueror from suffocation by wrenching him free from a battered faceplate that was choking off his air. In gratitude, William rechristened George as "Eyre"—"For ye have given me the eyre [air] I breathe.")

Despite the considerable depreciation of the nobility of our last name, these were adventures our children will never forget. They have walked the paths of their great-great-grandparents. They know something of their personalities and their courage.

We made up a private family book of narration and photos and called it "English Eyres and Swedish Swensons," and it's become a family treasure.

Families don't have to go to England and Sweden to accomplish the same identity-building discoveries. Some old family photos, maps of pertinent places, and stories from old diaries or journals can be the raw materials for creating a rich heritage of extended families, which can teach children both who they are and where they came from.

*T*he most miserable I can ever remember being was at about age twelve. I (Linda) had wonderful parents . . . though they weren't traditional. My mother, who married for the first time at thirty-eight, and my father, who had lost a wife to cancer and had married my mother at age fifty-two, were wonderful, caring, nurturing parents. My adopted brother and my sister and I were at the center of their lives, and we knew it. But my problem was that I didn't have any friends.

Painfully shy and wearing ugly salmon-colored cat-eye glasses, I found it very difficult to go to school. The worst were those stupid school dances where attendance was required! I would paste myself to the flowers on the wall and try not to be noticed. How I hated sitting all by myself during those horrible hours. Finally, on the eve of yet another dance, I became so concerned that I took the drastic step of sharing the problem with my mother.

Although in hindsight, as a mother myself, I now know my mother must have been stabbed in the heart when I stumbled through the story of my misery, she said in a very calm, matter-of-fact voice: "Linda, when you go to the dance tomorrow, I want you to try just one thing that I learned when I was a girl. When you go into the dance, look for someone who feels worse than you do. There will be somebody, I promise. Just find that person, think of some questions that will start a conversation, and go for it! Promise me you'll try that!" I finally did promise her, after she told me of a friend she once made by trying this herself.

I appreciated my mom's idea, though I still thought I had a better idea—which was just not to go. But I walked into the next seventh-grade, once-a-month, mandatory fifth-period dances mortified and certain that I could never find anyone more miserable than I was. Yet when I surveyed the room, sure enough, there she was. The thought of talking to her almost took my breath away. She was basically a social outcast. She had an unsightly skin condition and totally out-of-style hair and clothes. How can I talk to her? I thought. Then all the other kids will know for sure that I'm a loser too! But I'd promised my mother, and my mother had told me that she once did this same thing! I took a deep breath, got a couple of conversational questions in mind, and forced myself to sit down by her and start talking. It was the start of one of the best learning experiences—and the best friendships—of my life.

That breakthrough became part of the lure of our own family and part of the motivation of a lifelong effort to get our own children to climb out of their little comfort zones—not only when they aren't feeling confident themselves, but every day.

Several years ago we began having what we call "a huddle" at the front door just before the kids scoot out for school. With arms around one another, football huddle fashion, we say a simple prayer together for safety and for the ability to find someone that day who needs our help and to do something about it. We do it in honor of Grandma, who taught me the principle. Because of her, noticing others who need help has become a family tradition that helps our kids by taking their minds off their own self-doubts and insecurities.

If kids feel they are securely hooked together in a family root system that supports them and "holds them in place," it is so much easier for them to reach out and help others. The most cherished and rewarding stories we have heard have been not from our children, but about them: from other people who tell us about the day Talmadge came and sat by them at lunch when they were feeling alone or left out, or about the year when Saydi organized her neighborhood friends to meet for lunch every day at the locker of a girl whose life was out of control, so they could all talk together. That entangled root system can produce miracles!

Learn the Law of the Redwoods. Link and intertwine and completely immerse your dreams, your identity, and your destiny with the other members of your family. Support your children through things as small as attending their games and concerts to things as large as standing firm for moral principles and helping them plan their lives. Teach your children who they are! Hold them close physically and emotionally.

❖ ❖

One mother actually created an oil painting on canvas of a large tree that had three main branches—one for each of her small children—and four main roots that split to eight and then to sixteen. She put small photos of her children on the branches, of herself and her husband on the trunk, and of their parents, grandparents, and great-grandparents on the roots. She put the painting in the hall by the children's rooms and frequently told them stories about their ancestors, and those in particular that showed strong character traits like honesty or courage.

One wonderfully nurturing aunt who shared the parental responsibility with her single mom sister began to worry that the two elementary-age children thought their support system was limited to their mom and her. One Saturday she got out a big white poster board and helped the kids print a heading at the top: "People Who Love Me and Care About Me." With her help, the kids made a list on the chart that included godparents, an uncle, a grandmother, and three very special family friends who had known the children since their birth. She emphasized that there were others who loved and cared about the kids—special teachers, coaches, school coun-

selors, and lots of friends—but that the people on the poster-
board list were *family*. That they would always be there—all
their lives—to help and care for the children.

One couple, during a summer vacation, offered $50 to any of
their children who could recite by memory the names, birth-
days, and birth places of their grandparents, great-grandparents, and great-great-grandparents. There was a bonus of
another $25 if they could tell one story or incident they knew
about every one of those ancestors.

One single dad decided that the best way to give his son the
support and security the boy needed was to do his best to be there
for every key event or activity. Even though he only had his son
with him on weekends, he made a point of putting every ball
game or school assembly or recital on a big calendar in his kitchen,
to let his son know how important he was to his dad. When it was
absolutely impossible to be at something, he worked out a way to
have someone video the event so he could watch it later.

One father made copies of parts of his grandmother's jour-
nal (from her college years) and sent them to his daughters
at college.

One family created a family song, a family motto, and a
family flag to help increase the unity, identity, and security they
wanted the children to feel.

One family put together a small children's storybook containing little antidotes and incidents they had collected about their ancestors. There were two brief introductory stories. One was actually the story of redwoods and how the roots of other family members can interlock and strengthen us. The second was a story about an aunt in the family who as a teenager struggled with alcohol and depression but had the courage to share everything with her immediate and extended family. They linked arms (and hearts) with her and helped her stand and grow up through the storm.

One couple had two adopted children from Brazil along with their one biological child. They made a point of telling all three that they had chosen to bring each of them into their family and that they were exactly equal. When the two Brazilian children were old enough to understand, the couple explained that adoption meant "becoming totally a part of," and that they not only had adopted parents, but adopted grandparents, uncles, aunts, and ancestors. They also told their biological child that he not only had adopted siblings, but an adopted culture that was as beautiful and important and as much his as the U.S. culture.

The family celebrated both U.S. and Brazilian holidays, historical dates, traditions, and cuisine. All three kids grew up feeling that they had two strong and good sets of roots.

One family had picked up somewhere a certain aversion to what they called "PDAs" (Public Displays of Affection). The parents as well as the children had developed a pattern of being somewhat cynical and critical when it came to what the adolescent daughter called "the touchy-feely stuff" and what her younger brother called "mushy."

Then the family had a real scare when an older brother was involved in an accident and his condition and prognosis were unclear for a time. During the period of uncertainty there was a lot more hugging and hand-holding and touching going on among them, and they felt a much needed assurance and strength from the physical "intertwining." Later, even after the crisis was past and the injured brother recovered, the "touchy-feely stuff" continued, and continued to feel good. Tasteful "PDAs" became an acceptable part of the family's pattern.

One single mom found herself making negative comments about her ex-husband to her children when she became angry or disappointed with something he had done. Realizing that she was pointing out negative family traits from her husband's side of the family that could indirectly damage her kids' self-image, she decided that regardless of her feelings, she would portray his side of the family only in positive terms. His blood flowed in the children's veins, she reasoned, just as much as hers did.

One couple took the extra effort to organize the first extended family reunion they had ever held with grandparents, aunts, uncles, and cousins from both sides. Before the weekend affair, they helped their small children recognize the faces in photos and learn the names. At the reunion, each person told a couple of stories about themselves, and each adult made a special effort to explain to each child that they *cared* about them, that even though they didn't see one another often and in some cases hadn't even met, they were still *family,* and they would always be there for them.

One mother made a "shadow profile" poster of her four-year-old son by standing the boy up against a big poster board, shining a flashlight on him, and tracing the outline of the shadow that resulted on the poster. All around the profile the mom wrote the things she liked and admired about her son. She wrote them all in the language of "who you are," such as: "You are always so friendly with other kids . . . You are always willing to help when I ask . . . You are good at remembering to brush your teeth."

When her son was eight years old, the mom helped him make a list of "Decisions in Advance"—things he had already decided, like "I won't do drugs . . . I'll always tell my mother the truth . . . I won't cheat on tests . . . I'll care for the earth and not litter," and even, "I'll graduate from high school and go to college." She explained to the boy that the things he had decided were part of *who he was*. He was an honest person, he was a person who cared about his body and the earth and wouldn't abuse either, he was a college-bound person, and so on. Then she showed him his old four-year-old poster and reminded him that the things he had written then were also part of who he was.

That kind of talk became a real bond between them and gave the boy a secure sense of identity. Later, as a teenager, whenever he left the house, his mom would say, "I love you, son. Remember who you are!"

One dad, understanding that gratitude is an important part of security, took his two elementary-school boys to the downtown shelter one Saturday, having arranged to help serve a hot breakfast to several dozen homeless men. As he had hoped, the experience prompted a lot of talk about gratitude and blessings. But it did something more. The boys wanted to go back and help again. They began to think of themselves as givers rather than only as receivers.

Our family

What We Learn
from the Redwood Trees

❖

Redwood trees are the tallest living things on earth.
They grow in groves or families,
and their roots intertwine underground
as if they're holding hands.
In this way they support one another
and help one another stay straight and tall
even in huge winds and storms.
Our family can be the same way.
We hold on and help
and support one another
so nothing can bring us down.

Another meaning for the word "roots" is
our ancestors—our grandparents and
their parents and their parents.
Since we came from these people,
we inherited a lot of their qualities—
from their looks to
their personality traits.
As we get to know more about them,
it helps us know more about ourselves.

*S*o often we go to such extreme lengths as parents in our efforts to give our children security. We work long and hard to give them a big home and expensive clothes. Children's real security, though, doesn't come from these things. It comes from knowing who they are and where they came from. It comes from intertwined roots and from parents who prioritize them within homes that are emotional safe harbors from life's storms.

❖

REMEMBER THE LAW OF THE REDWOODS.
GIVE YOUR CHILDREN THE IDENTITY AND
SECURITY OF KNOWING WHO THEY ARE
AND WHERE THEY CAME FROM.
MAKE THE EFFORT TO LINK YOUR ROOTS
WITH THOSE OF OTHERS WHO LOVE YOUR KIDS.
KEEP YOUR GROVE GROWING STRAIGHT AND
TALL AND PROTECTED FROM
BOTH WIND AND ROT.

❖

7

The Nature of
RESPONSIBILITY

NOTE TO PARENTS: The next two natural laws (Chapters 7 and 8) apply principally to parents and to older kids. Some of the ideas in each chapter will work with younger children, but the opening animal allegories may be a little too graphic (and could be frightening) for children under 10.

By the time I (Richard) was in elementary school, my family had moved to a little town in the Rocky Mountains. There was a legend in that town—some said a true story, probably a combination of the two—about a huge grizzly bear known as "Old Ephraim" or "Old Three Toes" that had terrorized the early settlers of the community in the 1880s. Because of the legend, and because grizzlies still lived in the not-too-distant mountains, there was interest in the huge bears, and I grew up knowing a little about their size and their ferocity.

Even the name is scary—"grizzly" in the common vernacular, ursus arctos horribilis *in scientific jargon. Grizzlies get as big as seven feet and 800 pounds, and they have three-inch claws. Their unique muscle connections give them phenomenal strength in their jaws, shoulders, and front legs. They can eat 40 pounds of food per day and can outrun a deer over short distances.*

My own personal favorite story about a grizzly bear, however, is not the old legend, and it aims more at humor than at fear.

Two hikers were walking up a trail high in the Rocky Mountains one day, and as they came around a bend in the trail, they found themselves face-to-face with a huge bear. One of the hikers immediately sat down on the ground, pulled a pair of running shoes out of his backpack, and hurriedly began putting them on in place of his heavy climbing boots.

The other hiker stared at him in amazement and asked, "What are you doing? Do you think you can outrun a bear?"

The first hiker answered, "I don't need to outrun the bear; I just need to outrun *you!*"

Sorry about the slightly grizzly implication of the story, but its purpose is to make the point that we sometimes view our lives with the perspective of that first hiker, running away or trying to distance ourselves from difficult situations, and pegging our survival on our ability to outmaneuver or stay ahead of other people who will become victims.

For example, we might ignore the problems of the inner city or of a declining neighborhood because we don't live there anymore, we've escaped it. Let someone else get eaten! It's not our problem.

In our families, if we're not careful, we let our children avoid accountability in similar ways. They don't clean their rooms because they can run away from it—someone else will do it. They don't earn their own money because we will give it to them. They don't have to face up to or fix their own mistakes because we will bail them out.

And as parents, we have our own ways of running from or escaping difficult or unpleasant tasks—of leaving the tough battles to others. We imagine that we're on too fast a track to have time for our mundane, everyday parental duties, so we leave as many of them as we can to caregivers, schoolteachers, coaches, music teachers, tutors, camp counselors, and anyone else we can farm our kids out to. We adopt the "general contractor" method of parenting: using or hiring "subcontractors" to do the actual work of "building" or training or teaching our children. We begin to see our job as just lining things up and then getting our kids from one place to another.

Like the hiker in running shoes, we scramble for safer, higher ground, prioritizing our own comfort and leaving someone else to deal with the bearish burdens. Valuing extra status or wealth, we're willing to sprint ahead with our careers even when it means leaving the "burden" of a small child with a tender or at day care for extended periods. Then we let our kids return the favor when they escape from cleaning their rooms or doing household chores or budgeting their money.

Neither parents who delegate to day care because they can't afford not to work nor parents who hire household help because they can afford it should feel guilty. Indeed, they are both probably doing what they do for their children—to provide for them or to buy more time with them. But be careful not to go too far in either direction. Scaling back one parent's work to allow more time with a small child is always worth considering. And there are some deep benefits in doing many of the mundane tasks and responsibilities of a household yourself and with your children, even if you can afford not to. When you wash dishes or scrub floors, you not only set an example of work, you perform an act of love and self-reliance that children long remember and ultimately imitate.

The Law of the Bear is responsibility—taking full and complete responsibility for our families and for each of our children; prioritizing our parental role above our other roles; teaching our children by that example, and expecting them to accept family responsibilities too.

It is an important lesson because responsibility, like a fast, hungry bear, usually catches up with us. Running from family financial responsibility—living beyond our means—probably results in credit card debt that eats us. Running from the direct, everyday responsibility for small children results in lost opportunities to enjoy their childhood, and perhaps eventually results in less trust and communication, and in kids with expanding problems that we may not even know about. In addition, letting our children run from family and personal responsibility often results in adolescents who are always looking for the easy way out and who never become truly independent.

❖ ❖ ❖ ❖ ❖ ❖ ❖ ❖ ❖ ❖ ❖ ❖ ❖ ❖ ❖ ❖ ❖ ❖ ❖ ❖

Unlike the retreating hiker, we must face up to the full responsibility of raising a child, accepting the help of sources from schools to scouting, and even hiring help when we can afford it and when it gives us more time with the kids. But we must meanwhile always remember that "the buck stops here." No one can raise a child alone, and no one should try. We should graciously accept the support and assistance of other individuals and institutions. But parents need to be the "prime movers" as well as the "orchestrators."

Unlike   the retreating hiker, we need to prioritize the challenge in front of us, realizing, as C. S. Lewis said, that parenting is the ultimate career, and the career for which all other careers exist.

Unlike   the retreating hiker, our children need to confront responsibility of their own, from little household chores when they're small to earning their spending money during their teens.

❖ ❖

The beauty of family responsibility is that, as it is faced and accepted, it becomes a trained and loyal bear, a protective companion that makes our challenging child-rearing walk through the woods safer and more enjoyable. It allows us to keep moving forward on the path rather than running back up the hill or taking detours off into the underbrush. It becomes our friend rather than our foe, a loved member of the family rather than something to be avoided or feared.

As you thoughtfully give responsibility to your children, you are providing them with the opportunity to grow into the independent adults you want them to be. And, in the process of giving and accepting responsibility, *you* are becoming the complete and responsible adult *your* parents wanted you to be.

Several years ago while we were living in Washington, D.C., we were asked to a lovely dinner party in Georgetown. I (Linda) sat next to a woman who began to talk about her children. She said, rather absentmindedly, "I don't know what anyone does with a teenager. I just don't have a clue about my daughter. She's thirteen and she lives in her own world. What do you think about boarding school? It just seems like such a logical place for a teenager to be at an age when they want to be with their friends 24 hours a day anyway. Plus, it is so wonderful to have people right there with them who are really trained to deal with teenage problems."

As I asked her about other aspects of her life, she launched into an amazing story about her love for dogs. She had adopted several ailing pooches, nursed them back to health, and found good homes for them. And it seemed that most of her waking moments for the past few months had been spent preparing one of their thoroughbred dogs for a dog show. As it was just past the winter holidays, she was excited to tell me that for Christmas she had given her husband a handsome, beautifully framed 28- by 36-inch portrait of their favorite prize-winning dog.

I am in absolutely no position to judge this woman, but I do have to mention that when I asked to see a picture of her daughter toward the end of the evening, she couldn't find one in her purse, but she did pull out several lovely pictures of her dogs. I thought a lot about this mother in the next few days. Interestingly, she had helped me look at "the dogs" in my own life.

We all have those "dogs," which might account for an enormous amount of time when we do what we ourselves love, such as exercise, athletic events, or travel. There are also "dogs" that we don't love but feel compelled to take care of. That category could include projects at work, at church, or in the community. We could add obsessions to keep the house clean, never-ending phone calls, and remodeling or building a home. One or all of these "dogs" can obscure our ability to see that none bear comparison to taking full responsibility for guiding our child's life.

*M*any years ago we woke up one Saturday morning to a knocking on our bedroom door. We opened it to find four of our kids, ages seven through eleven, demanding their weekly allowance. Something about it didn't feel quite right, and we began to wonder if something-for-nothing allowances were the best way to go.

After a little thinking, a few discussions with the kids, and a lot of trial and error, we evolved a family "banking system" that served us well over the years because it emphasized initiative and responsibility and resembled the "real world" more accurately than an allowance system.

Each child had a simple peg board with his name on it and four big blocky pegs hanging from little chains. The first "morning peg" could be put in if he got up and was ready for school on time. The second "chore peg" went in when he'd done his assigned household task and checked the common area of the home or yard he'd been assigned to. The third "practice peg" could go in if he finished his homework and music practice. And the fourth "bedtime peg" was for getting ready for bed and being in bed by bedtime.

We made a big wooden "family bank," a box with a big padlock and a slot in the top into which the children could put a slip of paper each school night with a 1 2, 3, or 4 on it, depending on how many of their pegs they got in that day. To be official, the slip had to be initialed by the on-duty parent or caregiver. (By the way, when you take the time to set up a system like this, it's important for the sake of consistency that babysitters and tenders understand and implement it when you're away.)

Saturdays became "payday." The bank was opened by the paymaster (one of the two of us) and each child got paid according to how many total pegs he had for the week. One of the prime benefits of the system was that it gave us an opportunity to practice the Law of the Crabs. We would praise a child who had remembered his pegs and got "maximum money," and we'd try to simply ignore a child who did poorly.

As the system evolved, we gave the kids checkbooks (old or leftover "real" checks, but legal tender only at the family bank) so they could fill out deposit slips to put money in the family bank and write out checks to take money out. We adjusted the amounts the children could earn so they could begin to buy their own clothes. The bank included separate savings accounts, and the kids started taking 20 percent out of each "paycheck" for savings, along with 10 percent to give to church or charity. The family bank savings accounts paid high interest, with the stipulation that the savings and compounding interest could only be used for college tuition when the time came.

The best thing about the system is that it gave us frequent opportunities to talk about responsibility, self-discipline, and self-reliance. I think the day I really knew it was working was when I went into eight-year-old (and just barely "on the system") Noah's bedroom and discovered that for the first time in his life all of his clothes were hung up or neatly folded in his drawers. I must have shrugged or looked puzzled, because he came over, took my hand and said, "You know how expensive clothes are, Dad. That shirt right there was $26. I need to take care of my clothes so I can spend my money on other things."

Learn the Law of the Bear. Accept—and even relish—full responsibility for your family and children. Show respect for your child by giving him or her real responsibility.

❖ ❖

One family, concerned at how much time they were spending apart from one another, each involved in their own pursuits of work, schools, lessons, teams, and friends, decided to try two remedies. One was to set aside Monday nights as family nights, when they would all try to do something together—and to avoid scheduling anything that would keep them apart. The other remedy was to take their three children out of piano lessons, because the mom was a pianist, and out of tennis lessons, because the dad was a tennis player. For a year they decided to trade the accepted cliché, "You can't teach your own kids," for a couple extra hours spent together each week. For them it came to symbolize taking direct responsibility whenever they could, and prioritizing one another ahead of other pursuits or other people.

One family sat down together on a Sunday afternoon and made a simple list of all the things it took to keep the household going for a week —buying and cooking food, keeping the yard up, washing dishes—everything they could think of, until they had quite a long list. That led to a family discussion about how parents had *most* of the responsibilities but how children needed to feel involved by having *some*. Out of that discussion came the assignment of some specific household responsibilities to each child.

One single mother who heard about our peg board system accomplished the same thing in an even simpler way. She made up a basic star chart for each child, where each star represented a specific responsibility, such as cleaning their room or doing their chores. Instead of endlessly reminding the children to do each task, she could now simply say, "Are your stars up?" and the children could take the initiative of trying to remember what each of their daily responsibilities were. The mother also saw the value of tying the amount of each child's weekly allowance to how many stars he or she had put up for the week, so that the allowance was no longer an "entitlement" but a variable, proportionate weekly reward for the responsibilities that were met.

One family with preschoolers realized their kids were just too young to understand responsibility or to consistently remember to put away their clothes or toys. So the mom created an imaginative, "pre-responsibility game" that involved sewing eyes and a nose on an old laundry bag. The drawstring opening was the mouth, and the parents introduced the children to "Gunny Bag." They explained that he was a nice jolly guy who lived in the attic and that he had a strange habit. He liked to come down and "eat" any toys or clothes that were left out of place on the floor.

The idea worked like a dream! When Mom or Dad would yell, "I think I hear Gunny Bag coming," the kids went scurrying around putting things away before they could be eaten. Gunny would "cry and cry" because he couldn't find clothes or toys to eat. When he did eat something, he'd come back on Saturday and "cough it up" and the kids would quickly put it away so Gunny couldn't eat it again.

The "game" was fun for the parents and the children, and in the process the kids began to develop habits that would help them become more responsible as they got older.

One very religious couple, somewhat overwhelmed by the responsibility they felt for their beautiful but hyperactive twins, made a habit of praying for strength and guidance in their *stewardship* for two of God's children. They found that thinking of their children as a stewardship for which they were responsible to God gave them both humility and confidence.

One single dad whose sales job caused him to relocate frequently was dissatisfied with his daughter's academic progress but thought there was little he could do since she was forced to change schools every couple of years.

The girl seemed to readjust socially, but didn't do well with the academic transitions and thought of herself as a poor student.

Then one day the father happened to read a study that indicated that the most important variable in children's scholastic success was the involvement of their parents. Hoping that perhaps *he* could be the constant in her inconsistent academic life, he began to take more interest, ask more questions, and help more with homework. And he began to think of himself as being responsible for his daughter's education, rather than the principal, the teachers, or the school district. He helped her set scholastic goals for the school year and told her he was going to be there to help her reach them.

Her progress was immediate and dramatic.

One mom, hopeful of helping her nine- and eleven-year-old boys make responsible life choices, read about the "decisions in advance" approach (see Chapter 6). She adopted the idea, and put her own twist on it. She set up a chart for each of the boys, titled "Choices I Have Already Made." She explained to them that many people make bad choices and blame them on circumstances or the people around them. She explained that the worst time to make certain decisions is when you're facing them and there's pressure from people around you to do the wrong thing. She asked the boys, "When is the best time to make choices about things?"

Over the next few weeks she helped the boys come up with "premade choices" ranging from "I won't smoke" to "I won't ride with anyone who's been drinking" to "I'll stay a virgin throughout high school." (Different parents would encourage different decisions, but these were some that fit this family's values.) The boys initially listed their choices on the charts their mother made, signing and dating each entry so it became a kind of contract with themselves. As they got older, they copied their lists onto a private page at the back of their journals. Each time one of the boys wanted to add something to the list, mom would go through a "scenario" with them. ("You're at a party, everyone's trying a cigarette, and a girl you like gives you one and tries to light it for you. What do you say?") The case studies were like a dress rehearsal for the real thing.

One family with three basketball-crazy boys was having a difficult time getting them to remember to check on the part of the house or yard they had been asked to be responsible for . . . until the father started calling the assigned areas "zones." The boys knew all about "zone defense," and all dad had to say was, "Remember, a good defender doesn't let anything bad happen in his zone!"

One family decided to forgo their usual elaborate and expensive Christmas and instead use the holidays to go on a "service expedition" to a rural part of Mexico where they helped dig a well for a small, very poor village. The children, who went without any presents that year—having agreed to the trip instead—gained enormous perspective and gratitude through the experience and came to feel that in a small way they could do something about the "bear" of poverty rather than distancing themselves from it. The parents bonded with their children as they worked and served together, and they found that the trip actually cost less than their usual commercial Christmas.

Another family did a similar but less elaborate project at the local homeless shelter in their own community. In both cases powerful lessons were learned about the responsibility parents wanted their children to feel for humanity.

Our family

What We Learn from the Bear
♦

Some people, when they see a bear, try to run away
from it in hopes that it will eat someone else
instead of them. But bears are like responsibilities—
they'll catch you if you run, so it's best to face them
rather than run away.
In our family we all try to take responsibility for
the things that are important.
And we try to help other family members
with their responsibilities, without taking
the responsibility away from them.
Let's remind one another of the Law of the Bear!

*T*he problem many of us have with responsibility is procrasti-
nation. Parents say, "I'll spend more quality time with the kids
when I finish this project, get the promotion, move into a new
house." Kids say, "I'll do the dishes or clean my room after I practice, after my homework, after this TV show, or as soon as I can."
Of course everything can't happen right now, but we must remind
ourselves that every day with a child is precious, and that the extra
time it takes to set up patterns of responsibility pays off forever.

There are many ways to approach responsibility within a
family. What methods you choose is not nearly as important as

your commitment to the principle, and to the emphasis that your children see you putting on it. Start with the positive. Work on things *with* your children. Recognize the responsibility your child already takes, and give yourself some credit for *all* the responsibility you accept just by being a caring parent. Then look for ways to build on what you already have. Start with small steps, and be content with gradual progress and steady improvement, because parenting is not a game of perfect.

◆

REMEMBER THE LAW OF THE BEAR.
DON'T RUN. STAY. FULLY ACCEPT FAMILY RESPONSIBILITY
AND TURN IT INTO A JOY.
GIVE CHILDREN RESPONSIBILITY, WHICH IS
THE ULTIMATE INDICATION OF YOUR RESPECT FOR THEM.
MAKE RESPONSIBILITY A KEY WORD AND
A FREQUENT TOPIC OF CONVERSATION
WITHIN YOUR FAMILY. THERE ARE NO QUICK FIXES.
IT TAKES TIME AND PATIENCE, BUT ULTIMATELY,
RESPONSIBILITY BECOMES THE MEASURE OF OUR LIVES AND
OF OUR CHILDREN'S HAPPINESS.

◆

The Nature of AWARENESS

A dirt bike trail goes up into the hills behind a cabin in Idaho where we try to spend part of our summers. About the only thing the road leads to is a little moss-covered pond that has always been a hit with our children because it's just full of frogs. Our kids love to try to catch them, and they're endlessly amazed by how well the frogs swim and how far they can jump. A couple of our small boys became remarkably adept at imitating their musical "Rrrrribbit, rrrrribbit."

Frogs are amazing creatures. They've been around for 200 million years. They were here with the dinosaurs! They can be found on all seven continents. They live in deserts and in the tropics, at sea level and atop tall mountains. They're extremely adaptable animals. Much of their survival ability has to do with their remarkably long and strong rear legs, which enable them to jump more than 25 times their body length. But those same long, strong legs are considered a culinary delicacy by many humans. And what we want to talk about here—with apologies to the squeamish—is not how long frogs have existed or how high they can jump, but how they can be cooked!

A frog-leg-fancying friend once told us about the most fla-vor-enhancing method for cooking frog legs. The key to freshness and flavor, he explained, is to toss the frogs alive into the pot, similar to how lobsters are cooked. (And he insisted this is no less humane than any other way of turning them into food.) But with frogs it only works if you know exactly how to do it. If you put a live frog in boiling water, his lightning quick reflexes along with his jumping ability will catapult him immediately out of the pot. But if you put frogs into a pan of cool or lukewarm water they feel comfortable there, they relax and sit back in their natural watery environment and don't make much effort to escape.

Then you turn up the heat so gradually that the frogs don't notice what's happening until it's too late. They get so comfort-able they fall asleep, and before they wake up, they're cooked.

Let's think about that process—about what actually hap-pens in the phenomenon of cooking frogs: The frog is released into water, his natural environment, so he feels comfortable. It's his comfort zone. The water feels so familiar that he loses his sense of alarm or awareness of danger. His tendency is to think that water is water, that all water is the same, that water is safe.

Since he's cold-blooded, he's not very sensitive to the temperature of the water, so he doesn't really notice that the heat is gradually going up. In fact, as the water gets warmer, he feels even more comfortable and drowsy, until he's essentially immobilized, completely unaware of the danger. He falls asleep. Thus, before he feels the heat, it's too late; he's unconscious and unaware, and so he cooks.

Please excuse that slightly gruesome account, because it does make a powerful point. When we become too comfortable, too set in our routine, too busy with our work, we essentially fall asleep and lose our sensitivity and awareness, thus failing to notice either the signals of danger in our children or their unique potentials and the opportunities for positive action.

On average, how much time do you think goes by between the time a child first experiments with drugs and the time a parent becomes aware of the child's drug use? Over two years! *How many parents become aware of a problem—any kind of problem—only when it's too late to effectively do something about it? And it's not just negatives or problems—how about opportunities? How many parents notice a child's true gift or talent too late to effectively encourage or help him develop it?*

We can't help our children if we don't know what's happening to them. We can't help them avoid or overcome a problem if we don't see it coming or notice its warning signs. We can't help them develop a talent if we haven't noticed their gift or potential aptitude for it. We get in the busy routine or comfort zone of our own world and we don't probe or ask or notice enough to know what's really going on in our children's world . . . or in their minds or in their hearts.

The Law of the Frog is awareness! Awareness can be the greatest asset of parents. It can make us conscious of all the other laws, and capable of implementing and benefiting from them. And lack of awareness is what allows problems to get too big to handle and allows all kinds of opportunities to slip by unnoticed. When we're too much in our own rut or our own world, we don't notice much or feel much about our children's world. The signs may be all around us, the heat may be going up, but we just don't see it or feel it. We get a little sleepy and imagine that everything is fine.

The frog's good, natural instinct is to jump, and our good, natural instinct is to nurture and help our kids. Our instinct and our intentions are usually right. We get little nudges or feelings that something's not right with a child—or promptings that we should ask about some worry or pursue some potential or talent a child has. But we're so busy splashing around in our own comfort zone, and we're a little sleepy.

❖ ❖

U n l i k e   the frog, we must try harder to notice and feel and be aware of what's going on around us, and in our kids' lives and inside their heads.

U n l i k e   the frog, we must get out of our comfort zones and our assumption that all is well and nothing is changing with our children.

U n l i k e   the frog, we need to stay awake and alert and notice and pay early attention to both danger signs and manifestations of interests, talents, and opportunities.

U n l i k e   the frog, we have to understand that all water—all situations, all kids—are *not* the same, that each is different and that we have to understand those differences.

U n l i k e   the frog, we have to be warm-blooded— deeply interested and caring and sensitive to our children and their worries and concerns.

U n l i k e   the frog, we have to ask questions, lots of them—about where we are with our kids, where they are with their lives, what they're thinking, and what they need.

❖ ❖

One particular couple we used to know—we'll call them Val and Elaine—was just the opposite of many preoccupied and disinterested parents. They were a little *too* gung-ho, a little *too* caught up in their kids' lives. They were several years older than Linda and I, and their kids were teenagers when our first two were just toddlers.

Either Val or Elaine, or both of them, went to every activity that any of their three kids were in—every soccer game, every school assembly, every music or dance concert, every parent-teacher conference, every debate meet. Even, it seemed, every sleep-over, because the sleep-overs always seemed to be at their house. Elaine was like the Pied Piper or the mom in the Kool-Aid ads—the one that attracted all the other kids in the neighborhood, and the one they could all talk to. And Val didn't seem to mind driving a whole carload of thirteen-year-old friends down to the video store on a Friday night or over to McDonald's on a Saturday morning. I began to wonder if they had a life other than the one they lived with—and seemingly vicariously through—their kids.

But before I could get too critical or skeptical, I noticed how their own kids talked to them, and how the other kids who were always around talked to them. There didn't seem to be a generation gap. They'd talk about music, about TV, about what was cool and what wasn't. Kids talked to them like they were friends, and I envied what I saw.

As the years passed, we got to know them better, and because we admired their family and were so impressed with the kind of adults their children were becoming, we talked with Val and Elaine a few times about their parenting philosophy and approach. It turned out that they did indeed have active and intellectual lives separate and apart from their kids, and the things they did with their children were well-conceived—part of a strategy.

Basically, they told us that they thought the hardest part of parenting was knowing what was really going on—both the "outer stuff," like what their kids were doing and who they were hanging out with, and the "inner stuff," like what they were thinking and feeling. They had watched other families who had essentially lost their kids to drugs or gangs or just to a general sense of indifference and psychological separation, and they said they'd decided there were only three good sources of information or "intelligence." One was their kids themselves, another was their kids' friends, and the third was their teachers, coaches, counselors, or any other adults who spent time with them.

So they had consciously decided to be in their children's world and to ask and learn about the parts of their kids' lives that they couldn't see firsthand. They couldn't always go to everything, but they shared the load, Elaine going to some things, Val to others. Parent-teacher meetings, instead of one more obligation on the calendar, became an opportunity to find what teachers had noticed about their children. Driving or hosting their kids' friends became a chance to listen and ask and become interested in what their kids were thinking. And they didn't have to force themselves to act interested in their children, since they viewed interaction with them as the best and primary source of the very answers they were seeking.

I do wonder, even as I look back and admire Val and Elaine, if they gave up a little too much or if they limited their own world in order to be so involved in their children's. Maybe their approach can be modified or simplified, but the positive lesson is that they were right about the three sources that can help us really know our children, and that spending time and mental energy with each of the three is an opportunity as much as it's an obligation.

*I*t was obvious that our youngest daughter had musical ability and interest, because she basically started singing before she started talking. She would belt out her made-up tunes and attempted words with gusto and with an exaggerated vibrato.

As soon as we could find a one-eighth-size violin, I (Linda) got her started—after all, her sisters and I were violinists, and that was more or less the instrument of choice around our house.

Our little daughter liked the cute, miniviolin, and liked trying to play it. She was understandably terrible at it at first, but was less understandably terrible at it after months and then years of lessons. She still loved music and had a great sense of pitch, but she and the violin just didn't seem to click. We'd sit and cringe at her recitals, sometimes secretly hoping that the other parents wouldn't know whose daughter she was.

Finally we asked ourselves the unthinkable question: Was the violin really the right instrument for her? We thought about it and talked with her about other possibilities. It seemed wrong to waste those years of lessons and all the money they had cost, so we thought we ought to at least find something in the same clef so the music reading skills she'd acquired would continue to apply. I asked her if there was another instrument she'd like to try, and she said the flute. It occurred to me that, based on how much she talked, she would have plenty of breath for it.

It was a natural match. An instant love affair. Something about the flute was as natural to her as the violin was unnatural. Both she and we began to relish the practicing and the recitals as much as we'd dreaded them before.

All children have all kinds of natural talents, aptitudes, and interests that are a hidden part of them. Parents who *watch*, who *discuss*, and who cultivate an ever-growing *awareness* of who their kids are and what's deep within them can help children discover and cultivate their gifts.

Learn the Law of the Frog. Have the conscious goal of acute awareness regarding the feelings, the worries, the interests, and the situations of your child. Try not to assume and try not to be so optimistic that you're not realistic. Ask, probe, insist on knowing. Gather intelligence and insight from your child's friends and teachers. Cast your interest and "need to know" as a manifestation of your love.

✦ ✦

One single dad with weekend custody of his twelve-year-old son realized that he never got to see the boy in school or social situations. So he volunteered as an assistant coach for a Little League basketball team the boy wanted to play on with his friends. Though it cut down on the amount of individual time they spent together, the father discovered that he learned much more about his son and what he was thinking about by watching him interact with the other boys.

One couple went out to dinner once a month—just the two of them—with the sole intention of discussing their three children and brainstorming about how each child was doing and what each one needed. The idea was that if they shared their observations with each other, they would have some synergistic insights. One of them would have noticed something the other had missed, and discussing things together would prompt ideas about what to do.

These monthly discussions—always without friends or other distractions, and always with the agenda confined just to their kids—evolved into something they called a "Five Facet Review." They would ask each other, "How is Billy doing *physically?*" and discuss any observations or insights either of them had. Then, "How is he doing *socially?*" Then *mentally*, then *emotionally*, and then *spiritually*. They asked the same five questions about each of their children. They took notes and made plans and decided who would work on what. By the end of a monthly session, they had usually decided on three or four specific things to focus on together during the month ahead. Sometimes it was potential problems or worries they'd noticed or discovered—things they wanted to catch and change at an early stage. Other times their main focus was on opportunities or talents in their children that they wanted to develop or compliment.

Their collective observations—as they saw each child in varied situations—combined to create a synergistic feeling for what each child needed and common goals that they each could work on with each child.

One mom, despite how busy she was, started trying to say "Yes" every time she possibly could when her fourteen-year-old daughter and friends needed a ride somewhere. She found, like the family in the earlier story, that as the quiet chauffeur, listening and observing, she could pick up all kinds of things that were going on in her daughter's life (and in her daughter's *head*). Also—and this, too, came at some sacrifice—she encouraged the kids to make her home the weekend gathering place.

One dad discovered that his nine-year-old son seemed more open about what he was thinking and feeling if it was late at night and if he (the dad) practiced "active listening" instead of asking a lot of questions. He made a habit of putting his son to bed, "tucking him in," then sitting on the edge of the bed for a while and paraphrasing back whatever the boy said. If he said he had a bad day, the dad didn't say, "What happened?" He said, "Not such a good one today, huh?" If the boy said he'd had a fight with Billy, the dad didn't say, "What kind of fight?" or "Whose fault was it?" or "Do I need to call his dad?" Instead he just said, "Ah, so part of the bad day was the fight." And the boy went on, taking his own course through his thoughts and feelings, telling the dad far more than he'd have found out by asking his own questions. The "bedside chats" became something of a tradition and lasted well into the boy's teenage years.

One mom, who may have had a little too specific preconceived idea of what her small child could become, attended a parenting lecture one night largely because the advertised title intrigued her: "The Adventure of Mothering: Parenting by Discovery."

The speaker presented the premise that each child is a unique and complex mix of genetic factors that determine physical being and deeper emotional and spiritual qualities whose origins are not fully understood by anyone. "Every child is completely unique," he said, "and as any of you with two or more children can testify, the differences can be great even when the genetics are the same."

The lecturer went on to talk about how exciting and adventurous it can be for parents to make a conscious, concerted effort to discover who their children are—to search for the core and for the particular individual aptitudes, propensities, and potentials that each child has. "We need to spend more time and effort on knowing what we have," he concluded, "and tie our discoveries more closely into what we hope our children will become."

One dad got so tired of (and so worried about) his adolescent daughter's brush-off answers to his questions ("Fine" and "Okay") that he arranged to take her on a two-day business trip. His goal was to increase his awareness of her life. Indeed, away from home, without friends or distractions, she opened up more and he started getting solid answers to his questions and feeling some real connections to her life. He told her how much he wanted to know and share her feelings and her worries. He promised he would answer any questions she had as openly and honestly as he wanted her to answer his. On the flight home, they made a pact with each other that they called, "the open book." It just meant that they had no secrets, that they trusted each other, and that they wanted to share more in each other's lives.

One mom found that if she told her daughter little stories and recollections of how she felt when she was her daughter's age, it created a special bond and prompted the girl to share her own feelings and experiences more openly. The key was thinking of stories that showed she had some of the same problems and worries as her daughter—that she was just as real and as vulnerable when she was her daughter's age (none of the old, "I had to walk five miles in the snow uphill both ways").

One dad set aside an hour each Sunday—the one day he knew he'd be at home—to have a one-on-one "interview" with his eleven-year-old son. He anticipated that as the boy got older he might resist the interview format, but for now they both enjoyed it and the son seemed flattered by the dad's interest. Still, the dad was careful that his questions sounded like he was truly interested, rather than an interrogation, and he always followed a three-pronged format.

First, he asked questions relating to *character:* Do you feel like you're being honest? Is there anyone whose feelings you've hurt or who might not feel that you like them? Is there anyone who's offended you or who you feel a grudge against? What are the happiest things that happened this week? The saddest? The second category was *academics:* Which classes do you like best? The least? What tests are coming up this week? What can I help you on? The third category was *extracurricular:* How are you feeling about your basketball team? Are you going to try out for the school play? He wanted the order of his questions to suggest to his son the relative importance of the three.

Week by week, as the boy recognized his dad's sincerity, he opened up more and more. At the same time, the father became increasingly *aware* of his son's thoughts, feelings, and worries. And the sort of natural priority system the dad had hoped for was also formed. The son knew the most important things to his dad were the character issues, since they always came up first. And, though both were important, academics came before activities.

One family, in their effort to stay more aware of and interested in the children's lives, simply started trying to have dinner together more evenings. It was always a challenge to make dinner fit everyone's schedules, but on nights when they could do it, they played various verbal games around the dinner table, many of which were designed to draw out more of the kids' perspectives and feelings. They played "Interest," where each person would tell the most interesting thing he or she had seen or experienced during the day. They played "Speeches," where each person would stand and speak extemporaneously for one minute on a just-announced topic like "Friends" or "Things that bug me." They played "Similar," where kids would try to think of similarities between seemingly dissimilar things, like a telephone and a turtle (both have rounded surfaces, both start with a *t,* both would cease to function if a truck ran over them, and so on).

Our family

What We Learn from the Frog

❖

If frogs are in water that is getting
gradually warmer and warmer,
they don't notice the increasing temperature.
Then they fall asleep, and eventually
they get cooked.
Sometimes in families, things are happening
so gradually to children that they
don't really notice what they're getting into—
and their parents don't either!
We need to notice and be more aware of both
the good things and the bad things
that are gradually happening to us.
In our family, let's not be like the frogs.
Let's watch and notice worries and changes
and talents in one another.
And let's ask lots of questions so we really know
what one another is feeling and thinking.
That way nobody will fall asleep
and get cooked!

*I*t has been said that awareness is power. And in the absence
of awareness, little problems get bigger, and big problems
explode. It's hard to find a bad situation that couldn't have been

avoided or at least lessened or modified if there had been more awareness earlier.

We can never be aware enough to anticipate everything—to eliminate surprises altogether. But by making it a goal and constantly seeking it, our awareness of all aspects of our children can grow dramatically and become one of the most important assets a parent can have.

❖

REMEMBER THE LAW OF THE FROG.
DON'T GET TOO COMFORTABLE.
DON'T ASSUME ANYTHING.
BE MOTIVATED BY POSITIVE LOVE
RATHER THAN BY NEGATIVE SUSPICION,
BUT EXERCISE
YOUR RIGHT TO KNOW!

❖

9

The Nature of FREEDOM

Did you think the frogs from Chapter 8 were pretty amaz-
ing—broad-jumping 25 times their length? Then how
about a flea high-jumping more than 200 times its height?
Little $^1/_{32}$-inch fleas can jump or hop seven inches, and
they jump up and down so quickly and with such endurance
that they can complete 1000 hops in an hour. They can pull
an object weighing 100,000 times as much as they do. No
wonder "flea circuses" became a popular form of enter-
tainment in Europe in the nineteenth century.

As a small boy, when I (Richard) heard the term "flea
circus," I imagined flea clowns, flea trapeze artists, and flea
tightrope walkers. And indeed some of the turn-of-the-
century European insect extravaganzas did include elabo-
rate "acts" like this. But then one day I read, with some dis-
appointment, that most common, amateur flea circuses were

nothing more than a cigar box where fleas become conditioned to jump only as high as the lid of the box. After a while, when the lid is lifted, the fleas still hop up only to the exact height where the lid used to be. The "circus" is watching the pantomime of these little creatures bouncing around in the air as though there was a piece of glass over the box.

While it's not as cool as a flea on a tightrope, the phenomenon is still pretty interesting. The tiny fleas, with brains smaller than the point of a pin, nonetheless learn that they can only jump within the two- or three-inch vertical height of the inside of the cigar box. They develop the habit of confining their hops to exactly that level, and they hold to that habit and that perspective and that paradigm even long after the lid has been removed.

Children, unfortunately, often behave much the same. When there is a lid placed on their lives by parents who expose them only to one narrow slice of reality, they get used to that limited world, complete with its parochialism and prejudices, until it becomes a confining little box in which they live out the rest of their lives.

You might say, "Well, but there's media in that restricted space . . . so there's no way anyone today can grow up not knowing about the bigger world." And it's true that with all its dangers and drawbacks, media has shrunk our world and bridged wide gulfs of prejudice and propaganda. But it's not just knowing about the world that frees our children to fly above the box—it's knowing that they have the potential of incredible ver-

tical leaps. It's believing that the world and its possibilities are accessible *to them.*

The final law of nurturing is to let our children go, and to see that they go as high and as far as their true potential allows! There's a time to nurture and to hold close and safe and secure, and there's a time to take off the lid and encourage independent flight.

We didn't do a chapter on eagles, but they provide an interesting counterpart to the confined fleas. Mother eagles feather their nest with downy materials to make it as comforting and soft as possible for the eaglets, but when it is time for the young eagles to fly, Mom strips out the soft padding, making the nest prickly and uncomfortable. Then she pushes them out and makes them fly.

The Law of the Fleas is: Don't box them in for too long or put the lid too low.

This might seem a rerun of the Law of the Crabs—boost a child up rather than pull him back, praise instead of criticize, encourage his dreams, build his confidence and self-esteem. But that was about boosts; this is about potential, perspective, and long-range vision. This is about faith. This is about thinking and believing "outside the box." It involves little things like putting a world globe in a child's room, or taking him to soup kitchens to feed the home-less, or subscribing to *National Geographic,* or taking him to the Holocaust Museum. It involves bigger things like taking him to visit a variety of colleges while he's still a sophomore in high school, or going with him to talk to a guidance counselor about emerging new professions of the next decade, or taking a trip to a rural part of Mexico instead of to Disneyland. It involves ongoing and intensely important things like helping him discover his gifts and hidden potential and teaching him to think outside the box by being creative and doing things differ-ently than everyone else is doing them.

This law might appear contrary to the Law of the Redwoods, which is to stay in your grove and to bloom where you're plant-ed. Actually, it's the perfect companion law and corollary. We want our children to value and be protected by our home and our roots, but we also want them to grow tall enough to see out over the rest of the world and to sprout wings to get there.

There is also a harmony between this last law and the first one—the Law of the Geese. Become a citizen of the world so you can fly out far and away, with no limits—and *yet always come home.*

The Law of the Fleas is empowerment and freedom. None of us as parents know the full, individual, and unique potential of any one of our children, so it is our charge to do all we can to help each child discover who he is, what she can do, and where he can go. There is an "inner" and an "outer" aspect to this. We should help children look inside themselves and figure out what they're good at, what they love, and what they have passion for. And we should help them look outside themselves to notice both needs and opportunities, to see as big a picture as they can and to figure out where they fit into it.

❖ ❖

U n l i k e   the fleas, our children need to know that their childhood "box" was their temporary home, where they were nurtured not so they would stay, but so they could fly.

U n l i k e   the fleas in the circus, our children should perceive no roof or ceiling, no artificial limits to their happiness or their potential.

U n l i k e   the flea keeper, we should set no barriers or fences to their possibilities (behavioral limits— yes; barriers—no).

U n l i k e   the fleas, we don't want our children to conform and follow the same pattern as all the others.

U n l i k e   the fleas, we want them to think outside the box and to dream and to believe.

U n l i k e   the flea keeper, we need to give them the awareness of options and opportunities and the wide perspective that good dreams are made of.

❖ ❖

Remember that fear, overcautiousness, and self-limits are *not* things that children come with. They learn them from their parents' attitudes and behavior. The lids we put on them are made of our own excessive worry and lack of scope.

Most parents probably wouldn't think of "freedom" as a key element of parenting or as a goal for their families. But don't underestimate this ninth law. It's not something that was just tacked on the end. It may, in fact, be the culminating and ultimate law.

Consider these two perspectives on the word *freedom:*

1. *Freedom* as what we want our children to be "free to do." Free to dream, to set and reach goals. Free to develop their minds and talents and to reach their full potential. Freedom defined as empowerment and opportunity.

2. *Freedom* as what we want our children to be "free from." Free from violence or accident. Free from prejudice and mediocrity, from ignorance and error. Free from harm. Freedom defined as awareness and broad-mindedness, and as safety and protection.

Thus, this one word, *freedom,* may encompass our two most basic parental instincts and desires: to *protect* our children and to see them reach their fullest *potential.*

Yet there are also serious ironies in this ninth law. As parents, do we sometimes try to protect our children by taking away their freedom through curfews, grounding, and other rules? And do we also sometimes try to push them toward their potential by taking away their freedom? ("You can't go anywhere until your homework is done.") Does too much freedom work against their protection and their potential?

No! What rules, curfews, and other strong family policies take away is not freedom, it is *license*! Freedom is not about kids doing whatever they want whenever they want to. That is license, and most kids in developed countries have too much of it. License works against discipline, responsibility, security, and several other laws of this book. True freedom is about protection and potential and doing the hard things that lead to both.

To make our children free to live full lives and go to whatever place and level they wish to in this world, we must kindle their imaginations and make them *free to* dream. And then we must try to ensure that they're *free from* the things that would hold them back—to protect them not only from harm and physical danger, but from small-mindedness and stupidity, prejudice and parochialism, mediocrity and mistakes, ignorance and peer influence, accidents and acrimony.

Some protection may come from rules, beepers, close supervision, or even bodyguards, but the only real and *lasting* protection—and thus the only way to provide true freedom—is to teach our children values.

With that last sentence, we reveal a second reason why this book is a *prequel* to the book *Teaching Your Children Values*. (The first reason is that without the family atmosphere that the nine laws creates, we can't teach our kids much of anything.) The second reason is: True freedom is protection, and true protection means values. This is reflected in both the stories and the snapshots of this last law.

*T*he "lid" for some kids is inherently higher than it is for others. We have one daughter, Saydi, whose adventure meter is almost always off the charts. Of the seven of us who climbed to the summit, the 20,000-foot peak of Mount Kilimanjaro a few years ago, she was the one I (Linda) never doubted would make it. (Which is more than I could say about me!)

After high school, Saydi had been excited to leave her cozy high school world and go to Wellesley College in the Boston area, where she graduated in three years and then went on to do 18 months of humanitarian work and missionary service in Spain. Next she worked in Washington, D.C., for the Points of Light Foundation, and then went back to graduate school, where she got her master's degree in social work from Columbia University. While there, she worked in the trenches with welfare families in inner-city Manhattan, often in the most dire circumstances imaginable, all the while saying, *"I love my life!"* She was the first one on the pick and shovel as we helped with an irrigation system in remote Bolivia, and the first to "hit the mud" as we built a cistern on a humanitarian expedition in Africa (and the first to fearlessly scrape and bandage scabies sores on the legs of the village children). A wonderful boyfriend, who knew her pretty well, gave her the best birthday present she could imagine: a jump out of an airplane! (Parachute included.)

Then one summer she announced that this was the time she was going to live her lifelong dream of going to India to work in an orphanage. She didn't know why she felt compelled to go, but ever since she was a little child, she had nurtured that dream in her heart. At first she thought she would just go to India on her own. Sorry, that was when I snapped the lid of the flea box shut and said, "Forget it." But she didn't seem to hear me. She found funding and two friends to go with her. She found an orphanage in Madras run by an elderly couple who were taking in homeless children from the street. Even though I thought I was probably crazy, I finally gave up my objections and sent her off, backpack and all.

We worried about her for weeks, until she was able to find a run-down Internet café to let us know that she was still alive. She admitted from time to time that this experience was "much more" than she could have ever imagined or bargained for, and she sent heartbreaking stories of valiant children going on without parents and without anything in the world, and amazing old women whom society had cast aside and who they were able to recruit to come in and to help with the children. In 105 degree heat and 99 percent humidity, she and her friends turned a big, beat-up old garage into a newly painted, licensed refuge for orphans and castaways.

Many thanks were sent to heaven upon her safe return. Recently, when I came across the little diary where Saydi had kept notes on her trip, I reflected on how close we came to not allowing her to have that incredible, life-changing experience. In the diary, I found a list of things she had listed under the title, "Things I Am Thankful For." A few items from this *very* long list included: a good mattress, showers, plumbing and hot water, a garbage-collecting system, traffic laws, education, women's upward mobility and rights, love in marriage, good smells, Western toilets and toilet paper, salad, the fact that child abuse is illegal in America, customer service, the ability to do things efficiently, the absence of constant horns honking, communication and the ability to understand one another, medication, less pollution, hope for a better world, and *freedom*!

There cannot be a better feeling than to send out a little "flea" to discover that sometimes the world really doesn't have a lid. Given the chance to pursue dreams, there are more things to explore and learn and grow from than we can possibly imagine. Ah, that Richard and I could get out of *our* box and be more like Saydi!

*T*he story of *Teaching Your Children Values* is basically this: We found that virtually all parents, irrespective of religious, political, or cultural difference, wanted the same basic values for their children.

(A pretty good definition of a conservative is "a liberal with a teenage daughter.") But creating the common values list was easier than implementing it. Parents needed help with exactly *how* to effectively teach fundamental values to their kids. We were able to attempt a "how to" book largely because we had the advantage and blessing of being able to draw ideas from the tens of thousands of parents who were members of our parents co-op around the world *(www.valuesparenting.com)*.

Rather than throw all the values and all the ideas out to parents at once, we decided to try to get everyone to focus on one specific value during each month of the year, and then to flood them each month with ideas on how to teach that one particular value to kids of various ages. We sequence the values as shown on the following pages. (Individual parents, of course, revise and reemphasize according to their own beliefs and priorities.)

This list is just a starting point and an example of how to set up a value-of-the-month program in a family.

JANUARY: THE VALUE OF HONESTY
Honesty with other individuals, with institutions, with society, with self. The inner strength and confidence that is bred by exacting truthfulness, trustworthiness, and integrity.

FEBRUARY: THE VALUE OF LOVE
Individual and personal caring that goes both beneath and beyond loyalty and respect. Love for friends, neighbors,

even adversaries. And a prioritized, lifelong commitment of love for family.

MARCH: THE VALUE OF PEACEABILITY

Calmness. Peacefulness. Serenity. Holding to convictions but trying to accommodate rather than argue. The understanding that differences are seldom resolved through conflict, and that meanness in others is an indication of *their* problem or insecurity and thus of their need for your understanding. The ability to understand how others feel rather than simply reacting to them. Control of temper.

APRIL: THE VALUE OF SELF-RELIANCE AND POTENTIAL

Individuality. Awareness and development of gifts and uniqueness. Taking responsibility for your own actions. Overcoming the tendency to blame others for difficulties. Commitment to personal excellence.

MAY: THE VALUE OF SELF-DISCIPLINE AND MODERATION

Physical, mental, and financial self-discipline. Moderation in speaking, in eating, in exercising. The controlling and bridling of one's own appetites. Understanding the limits of body and mind. Being wary of the dangers of extremist viewpoints. The ability to balance self-discipline with spontaneity.

JUNE: THE VALUE OF FIDELITY, CHASTITY, AND COMMITMENT

Commitment to the security of fidelity within marriage and to the wisdom of restraint and limits before marriage. An understanding of the responsibility that goes with marriage and that should go with sex. Awareness of the long-range (and widespread) consequences that can result from sexual irresponsibility and infidelity.

JULY: THE VALUE OF LOYALTY AND DEPENDABILITY

Loyalty to family, to employers, to country, church, schools, and other organizations and institutions to which commitments are made. Support, service, contribution. Reliability and consistency in doing what you say you will do.

AUGUST: THE VALUE OF RESPECT

Respect for life, for property, for parents, for elders, for nature, and for the beliefs and rights of others. Courtesy, politeness, manners, and the avoidance of criticism and judgment.

SEPTEMBER: THE VALUE OF COURAGE

Daring to attempt difficult things that are good. Strength not to follow the crowd, to say no and mean it and influence others by it. Being true to convictions and following good impulses even when they are unpopular or inconvenient. The boldness to be outgoing and friendly.

OCTOBER: THE VALUE OF JUSTICE AND MERCY

Obedience to law, fairness in work and play. An understanding of natural consequences. A grasp of mercy and forgiveness, and an understanding of the futility (and bitter poison) of carrying a grudge.

NOVEMBER: THE VALUE OF KINDNESS AND FRIENDLINESS

Awareness that being kind and considerate is more admirable than being tough or strong. The tendency to understand rather than confront. Gentleness, particularly toward those who are younger or weaker. The ability to make and keep friends. Helpfulness. Cheerfulness.

DECEMBER: THE VALUE OF UNSELFISHNESS AND SENSITIVITY

Becoming more extra-centered and less self-centered. Learning to feel with and for others. Empathy, tolerance, and extra-centeredness. Sensitivity to needs in people and situations. Experiencing and understanding the joy of giving.

Besides being an end in themselves, each of these values can empower our children to reach their potential and can protect them from the mistakes, accidents, and other harm that they're more subject to in the absence of these values. By protecting and empowering, these values and their conscious emphasis within our families become the essence of true freedom.

Learn the Law of the Fleas. Empower and embolden your children to become true "citizens of the world" and to reach their fullest and most unique potential.

* *

One family (in fact, hundreds of thousands of families through our earlier book, *Teaching Your Children Values,* and the resulting *www.valuesparenting.com* Web site) simply decided to focus on one basic value each month, and then at the end of the year to start over and concentrate on those same 12 values the next year, and the next, and the next. Each one of their children, therefore, was focused on *honesty* for a full month when they were five, again when they were six, again when they were seven, and so on. And they did the same with each of the other 11 values. The cumulative effect of these focused month-to-month efforts is substantial: It protects the children in emotional as well as physical ways as they grow up, and when they leave home, it turns them loose on the world as moral and principled people.

One family with kids nine, eleven, and fourteen had a "world night" once a month. They went to a restaurant with a name starting with A one month, B the next month, and so on. The "ticket" each family member needed in order to go along was some computer research about the country or city or other world destination he'd most like to visit that started with that letter. At dinner, each family member, including Mom and Dad, would tell what they'd learned about Aruba, or Angkor Wat, or Adelaide, why they'd like to visit, and what they would do while there.

One mom, anxious to use her limited vacation time on something more memorable and relationship-oriented than the typical summer vacations at theme parks, found a humanitarian organization that sent "expeditions" to Third World locations to help with irrigation, education, or health-care projects. She and her two daughters went on an expedition to a mountain village in central Mexico and helped build an adobe health clinic. The experience dramatically changed the family's (particularly the children's) perspective on the world, opening a whole new vision of gratitude and the desire to give help and service. Interestingly, the trip actually ended up costing less than their typical entertainment-oriented vacations.

One dad, in an attempt to encourage a timid child to try more things, sat down with his son and put together an "adventure list" of things the boy thought he'd like to try some day. It included some pretty basic things like "hiking up Fiddlers Mountain," "diving off the high dive," and "skateboarding." As the list developed, it began to include some pretty exotic things, like "fly a pontoon plane" and "visit China." As the list grew, the father emphasized that the boy didn't need to try everything all at once, but he could *think* about things, and that there would eventually be opportunities to do them. It gave him frequent reason to say, "You know, you can really do anything you want to!"

The dad also made a "What I'm Good At" chart, where he could contribute to the boy's confidence by listing anything, big or small, that his son ever showed promise or interest in.

One mother who also had a very shy child found that her daughter was much less shy in her own home. So they tried to have friends over more often, so the girl could feel more comfortable and outgoing.

One family started a tradition of having a "guess who's coming to dinner" night once a month, where they would invite someone from a different and distinctive cultural background to have dinner with them. The children were expected to have a list of questions for the guest.

One couple (representing millions of parents who have learned the same lesson) found that *reading* is the password to everywhere and the key that unlocks all local limits. They began the habit of reading aloud to their children when they were very small, and continued the tradition as they grew, often with the children as the readers. They tried to find the time to go to the library together once every month to choose the books for the month ahead, focusing on novels and biographies set in circumstances and settings very different from their own.

One single mom, living in a relatively small town, discovered that she could get the *New York Times* delivered to her house for a fairly nominal rate. She and her two adolescent daughters started a ritual of each "reporting" at the dinner table on one article that interested them from that day's paper.

One father, anxious to have more dialogue with his children on the subject of values and character, set up a contest between himself and his three teenage kids. Each took one of the world's largest religions (one took Christianity, one Islam, one Hinduism, and one Buddhism) and went on the Internet to get some background on the values or rules of behavior advocated by that religion. Whoever participated would get to go on a family outing to nearby Yosemite Park. Everyone "qualified," and the outing became a prolonged discussion of values, leading to some conclusions about how universal certain basic values were and why they seemed to endure and to "work" so well worldwide.

One single man, who was more like a godfather or third parent to his three nephews, developed a tradition of asking them every month, "What do you want to be when you grow up?" He encouraged the kids to give him a *different* answer each month, and told them there were so many interesting things "to be" that most kids never even thought of. He promised them that whenever they thought of a new profession they might like, he'd try to take them (one-on-one) somewhere they could learn more about that particular type of job. When a child said "a fireman" or "a doctor," he would take them to a firehouse or a hospital for a visit. When one of his nephews said something like "an astronaut" or "President of the United States," he would at least take them to the library to look at books or pictures. The kids soon learned that the more interesting professions they could think of, the more interesting outings they would get with their uncle.

Our family

_____

_____

_____

_____

_____

What We Learn from the Fleas
❖

Tiny fleas can hop six or seven inches straight up,
but after they've been in a shallow box
with a lid for a while,
they learn to never hop higher than the lid.
Even when the lid is opened or taken off,
the fleas still only jump as high
as where the lid used to be.

People can be a little like the fleas,
thinking they have limits—
thinking they have to stay in the box.
In our family, we don't want
to have any lids on our potential.
We want to set high goals and
reach them and to keep learning and
progressing all our lives.
We want to have no box around us.
We want to experience
as much as we can about the world, and
to share and be of service to
people and places
that have less than we do.

*P*erhaps what all thoughtful parents want is for their children to live "out of the box," yet to preserve and hold their values firmly in hand no matter how far they go or how high they jump. While we can't ultimately control either their course or their destination, we can broaden their horizons, show them the options, and point out the paths.

❖

REMEMBER THE LAW OF THE FLEAS.
REMEMBER THAT
THE FINAL STEP IN NURTURING
IS TO LET THEM GO.

❖

THE SUBCONSCIOUS AND THE SYMBOLIC

Our goal as writers (and hopefully yours as readers) was not just to review a few principles you already knew, or to give cute new names to old ideas, or to perform some kind of quick fix on your nurturing ability as a parent. The goal was to help us all *focus* on, *remember,* and *practice* what we believe are the nine most natural laws of good parenting and of strong, healthy families.

We want this book's success to be measured not by how much you enjoyed reading it or by how impressed you may have been with some of its ideas. Rather, it is a success if you find yourself still aware of and still acting in accordance with the nine natural laws a year from now.

Your conscious mind, which you used to read this book, is going to be too busy with other things in the weeks and months ahead to stay focused on the nine natural laws every day. But your subconscious mind—that vast and largely undirected resource—can be your key. If you can get whales and crabs and elephant trunks well enough established in that powerful subconscious, it will begin to make your good parenting instincts and behavior as automatic as your digestion.

The subconscious mind can be programmed by symbols and images. Right now you can say "Geese" and think of commitment, or "Frogs" and think of awareness. But with time, these images and the details they symbolize will begin to fade. Therefore, we suggest three things:

1. Set this book out somewhere where you'll see it. Let its cover provide a subliminal reminder. Pick the book up occasionally and thumb through it. See if the images still remind you of the characteristics you want to exhibit as a parent.

2. Periodically—every few months or whenever the meaning of the symbols begins to fade—find an hour or two and reread just the allegories that open each of the nine chapters. Check yourself on your own ideas that you wrote in toward the end of each chapter; then add to them or write new ideas. Give a little booster shot to your subconscious, and then trust it to work for you and to influence your family actions and reactions.

3. Make your thoughts interactive by expressing your own ideas on and your experiences with the nine natural laws. Do this by going online to *www.valuesparenting.com* and clicking on the "nurturing" button. Your ideas will help other parents, and their ideas will help you.

Keep in mind, too, that this book is a *prequel* to *Teaching Your Children Values*—a book that will help you teach specific values within the more trusting and nurturing family environment you are now creating. We've put the 12 values from that book (listed in Chapter 9 of this book) into many forms (tapes, stories, lesson plans, etc.) to make them easier for both parents and children to assimilate. Get them at *www.values parenting.com*. If you're not yet a cyber person, call us at 801-581-0112 and we'll mail you the same stuff.

❖ ❖ ❖ ❖ ❖ ❖ ❖ ❖ ❖ ❖ ❖ ❖ ❖ ❖ ❖ ❖ ❖ ❖ ❖ ❖

You may have noticed that each chapter ended with a summary that started with the word "Remember." Let us end the book the same way:

R e m e m b e r   that your children are your top priority and your highest joy.

R e m e m b e r   that your children will be in your home for only about a fourth of your life (and a fourth of their life).

Remember to be natural and to trust your instincts.

Remember to enjoy your kids!

Remember that nurturing is the most important work you will ever do!

Remember that you are not alone in the concerns you feel for your children and your desire to become a better nurturer. There are tens of thousands of other parents whose concerns have been similarly focused by this book.

Remember to visit and stay in touch with these other points (and with us) at *www.values parenting.com*.

Remember the nine laws.

❖ ❖

Acknowledgments

We have been fortunate to work on this book with people who actually make clichés meaningful:

Our agent, Jan Miller,
who always goes the extra mile

Our editor, Nancy Hancock,
who knows the difference between good and best

Our illustrator, Von Fedoroff,
whose pictures really are worth a thousand words

About the Authors

Parents of nine children ("one of every kind"), Linda and Richard Eyre are the authors of the *New York Times* #1 bestseller *Teaching Your Children Values.* As network television parenting experts, White House appointees for family issues, international lecturers, authors of a dozen books on parenting, and founders of a global parents organization, they have devoted much of their professional lives to strengthening families.

The Eyres lecture throughout the world on parenting, lifebalance, and family-centered lifestyles and can be contacted at 801-581-0112 or at *www.valuesparenting.com.*

Other Books by the Authors

Teaching Your Children Values
Teaching Your Children Responsibility
Teaching Your Children Joy
How to Talk to Your Child About Sex
Three Steps to a Strong Family
Lifebalance
Life Before Life
I Didn't Plan to Be a Witch
A Joyful Mother of Children
Stories to Teach Children Joy
Empty-Nest Parenting
The Happy Family: Restoring the Eleven Essential Elements
Alexander's Amazing Adventures (Audiotape Series)